WILLA CATHER
A Checklist of Her Published Writing

WILLA CATHER
A Checklist of
Her Published Writing

Compiled by
JoAnna Lathrop

UNIVERSITY OF NEBRASKA PRESS · LINCOLN

Library of Congress Cataloging in Publication Data

Lathrop, JoAnna, 1931–
   Willa Cather : a checklist of her published writing.

   1. Cather, Willa Sibert, 1873–1947—Bibliography.
Z8155.65.L37   016.813'5'2   74–82561
ISBN 0–8032–5808–9 pbk.

Contents

Introduction

It is not the least unusual feature of Willa Cather's extraordinary career that today, almost three decades after her death, after numerous and widespread observances of the centenary of her birth (which included the issuance of a Willa Cather commemorative stamp), after a score of biographical and critical volumes and countless articles, reviews, dissertations, and theses devoted to her work, there is still no definitive Cather bibliography and—what is more—no immediate prospect of one.

Why should this be so? One reason that might be advanced is the duration of her literary career, which spanned nearly fifty years; another is the heterogeneous character and scope of that career—Willa Cather was a newspaperwoman (columnist, drama and music critic, book reviewer, reporter), a feature writer for magazines, an editor, poet, short-story writer, essayist, and novelist. Moreover, particularly during her first two decades as a professional writer, her work more often than not was unsigned or appeared under a bewildering variety of pseudonyms. Finally, and quite apart from these problems, the author herself created difficulties for the bibliographer. In Bernice Slote's words, "We have not known the extent of Willa Cather's accomplishments, partly because she did not talk about them. An experienced writer does not boast of routine accomplishment, or even remember it all. And for her, as time went by, it became unimportant to talk of past successes when greater ones were at hand. But she was reluctant to speak of practice sketches that had developed into major fiction. As she saw it, one's several careers could be separated and only the chosen be remembered."[1] Indeed, we know from E. K. Brown that Miss Cather actively disliked to be reminded of her early stories: "She was glad that she had the copyright and could prevent the republication of any among them. She compared her attitude to that of an apple-grower careful of his reputation: the fruit that was below standard must be left forgotten on the ground; only the sound apples should be collected."[2]

Presumably, if Miss Cather had had her way, the Cather canon would be limited to the work she chose for inclusion in the Library Edition of her works published by Houghton Mifflin (1937–1941). But, as Willard Thorp has written, "Posterity wishes to know and has ways of finding out by what stages a great writer proceeds to excellence."[3] As early as 1943, Benjamin D. Hitz had asked Flora Bullock, a fellow-student of Willa Cather at the University of Nebraska, to compile a bibliography of Miss Cather's early writing; completed in 1945, it was deposited in the Hitz Collection at the Newberry Library, Chicago, Illinois. In 1946 Mildred R. Bennett, in Red Cloud, Nebraska, began to research and collect Cather materials; and during the late 1940s and 1950s other scholars—among them James R. Shively, George Seibel, John P. Hinz, Harry Finestone, and Curtis Bradford—addressed themselves to the problems of unearthing and identifying the early work.[4] In 1956 Phyllis Martin

1. *The Kingdom of Art: Willa Cather's First Principles and Critical Statements, 1893–1896*, selected and edited with two essays and a commentary by Bernice Slote (Lincoln: University of Nebraska Press, 1966), p. 3.

2. E. K. Brown, completed by Leon Edel, *Willa Cather: A Critical Biography* (New York: Alfred A. Knopf, 1953), p. 145.

3. Statement to the University of Nebraska Press, 28 October 1965.

4. The author of *The World of Willa Cather* (New York: Dodd, Mead, 1951), Mildred R. Bennett also selected and provided a commentary for *Early Stories of Willa Cather* (New York: Dodd, Mead, 1957); even earlier she had identified a number of pseudonymous

Hutchinson published a bibliography in the *Bulletin of the New York Public Library* (June–August) which included nearly all of Miss Cather's signed publications identified up to that time exclusive of newspaper writing, as well as notes on editions and translations and an annotated though partial list of criticism.

A major impetus to further investigation came early in the next decade when the University of Nebraska Press embarked on the project of collecting and publishing Willa Cather's early writings. Bernice Slote, professor of English, University of Nebraska–Lincoln, and Virginia Faulkner, editor of the University of Nebraska Press, already had begun working with Mrs. Bennett. In 1961 the Press had published a new edition, with notes and an index, of Mrs. Bennett's *The World of Willa Cather* (see footnote 4), and Mrs. Bennett made available the archives of the Willa Cather Pioneer Memorial and Educational Foundation. The archives of the Nebraska State Historical Society also included much important primary material as well as a microfilm of the Bullock bibliography.

The first volume of the series, *April Twilights (1903)* by Willa Cather, edited with an introduction by Bernice Slote (Lincoln: University of Nebraska Press, 1962; revised edition

---

pieces, among them "When I Knew Stephen Crane," first reprinted in *Prairie Schooner* 23 (Fall 1949): 231–36. The letters, first editions, and artifacts which she began to collect in the mid-1940s are now in the archives of the Willa Cather Pioneer Memorial and Educational Foundation, of which Mrs. Bennett is co-founder and president. James R. Shively edited, introduced, and annotated *Writings from Willa Cather's Campus Years* (Lincoln: University of Nebraska Press, 1950). The late George Seibel wrote a valuable reminiscence, "Miss Willa Cather from Nebraska," *New Colophon* 2 (September 1949): 195–208. John P. Hinz included an extensive discussion on the pseudonymous writings in "Willa Cather in Pittsburgh," *New Colophon* 3 (1950): 198–207. Harry Finestone is the author of "Willa Cather's Apprenticeship" (Unpublished doctoral dissertation; University of Chicago, 1953); and Curtis Bradford contributed a helpful article, "Willa Cather's Uncollected Short Stories," *American Literature* 26 (January 1955): 537–51. Another early and useful bibliographical study is Frederic B. Adams, Jr.'s "Willa Cather / Early Years: Trial and Error," *Colophon* 3 (September 1939): 89–100.

1968), included the first complete bibliography of Cather's poetry. *Willa Cather's Collected Short Fiction, 1892–1912*, edited by Virginia Faulkner with an introduction by Mildred R. Bennett (Lincoln: University of Nebraska Press, 1965; revised edition 1970), included a complete bibliography of all the known stories for the period covered by the volume and a checklist of the later short fiction. What was probably the most important breakthrough in the study of Willa Cather came in 1964 and 1965 when Bernice Slote discovered "a body of writing which nearly doubled the number of items given in existing bibliographies of the Nebraska years, . . . and some unexpected biographical facts to piece together. The supposed year of inactivity and silence before Willa Cather left Nebraska for Pittsburgh in June of 1896 did not exist, and the gap between her journalistic writing as a student and the signed columns she sent back to the Lincoln papers from 1896 to 1900 was filled with material that made a continuous, interrelated sequence of comment on the arts." [5] The "unexpected biographical facts" led to further discoveries about Cather's activities as a journalist and free-lance writer in the East and to the uncovering of many additional Cather items. The first fruit of these findings was *The Kingdom of Art: Willa Cather's First Principles and Critical Statements, 1893–1896*, edited with two essays and a commentary by Bernice Slote (Lincoln: University of Nebraska Press, 1966). At the same time William M. Curtin, then at the University of Illinois, now an associate professor of English at the University of Connecticut, was working on a more extensive collection of the journalistic writings. Edited and with a commentary by Mr. Curtin, it appeared in two volumes under the title *The World and the Parish: Willa Cather's Articles and Reviews, 1893–1902* (Lincoln: University of Nebraska Press, 1970).

In the foreword to that collection the publishers stated that in 1964 they had realized that "the research into the early years, which we had assumed was virtually complete, was only beginning," and that although they had expected to conclude the series with the publication of *The World and the Parish*,

---

5. *The Kingdom of Art*, p. vii.

they had "underestimated Miss Cather." Consequently, they were postponing the full-dress bibliography they had originally planned and hoped to bring out a checklist as an interim measure. The wisdom of this decision has since been demonstrated, for new Cather writings continue to emerge. Some have been reported by Bernice Slote in her essay "Willa Cather," in *Fifteen Modern American Authors: A Review of Research and Criticism*, edited by Jackson R. Bryer (Durham, N.C.: Duke University Press, 1969), with additional findings included in the revised edition of that volume entitled *Sixteen Modern American Authors*, published by Duke in 1973 (also available in a paper edition published by W. W. Norton). A variant version of one of Cather's most famous stories, "Coming, Aphrodite!," which appeared in *Smart Set* as "Coming, Eden Bower!," was reprinted in *Uncle Valentine and Other Stories: Willa Cather's Uncollected Short Fiction, 1915–1929*, edited with an introduction by Bernice Slote (Lincoln: University of Nebraska Press, 1973), and other newly discovered items have been reprinted in the *Willa Cather Pioneer Memorial Newsletter*, *Prairie Schooner*, and *Vogue*.

It can be said with confidence that still more of Willa Cather's submerged work will be proved and reprinted in the next few years. Perhaps by the end of this decade it will at last be possible to start on a definitive bibliography. Until that time it is hoped that *Willa Cather: A Checklist of Her Published Writing* will perform at least some of the services of such a volume. It compiles (and in a few instances corrects) the bibliographies from *April Twilights* (1903); *Willa Cather's Collected Short Fiction, 1892–1912*; *The Kingdom of Art*; and *The World and the Parish*. It adds items previously not listed in any of these sources, and subsequent reprintings previously unlisted in other sources. The Phyllis Martin Hutchinson bibliography from the *Bulletin of the New York Public Library* was used to add information about essays and novels and to confirm items from other bibliographies. The Slote essay on Willa Cather in *Sixteen Modern Authors* was also used; and reprintings have been added from such periodicals as *American Heritage* and *Horizon* as well as those mentioned earlier.

Inclusions and Exclusions

Willa Cather: A Checklist of Her Published Writing records only English-language printings and reprintings published in the United States. It is intended primarily as a guide for scholars and students, rather than for book collectors; thus, although it includes special editions issued subsequent to the first edition (for example, the 1929 illustrated edition of *Death Comes for the Archbishop* and the 1973 Centennial Edition of *A Lost Lady*), it does not list limited editions which appeared simultaneously with trade first editions (as, for example, numbered and signed editions on special paper of *One of Ours, A Lost Lady, My Mortal Enemy, Obscure Destinies, Lucy Gayheart,* and *Sapphira and the Slave Girl*). Nor does it attempt to give a complete listing for the frequent textbook and anthology reprintings of certain short stories: "Paul's Case," "The Sculptor's Funeral," "A Wagner Matinee," and "Neighbour Rosicky." It lists Armed Forces and large-type editions, but not Braille editions.

The volumes collecting Willa Cather's early newspaper and magazine writing, *The Kingdom of Art* and *The World and the Parish*, include many cross references both within their commentaries and annexed to entries in their bibliographies. While they were essential to establish authorship, such cross references do not serve the purpose of this Checklist and they have been omitted. The scholar who is interested in the tests to establish authorship or who wishes to make textual comparisons should consult *The Kingdom of Art* (especially pp. 457–77) and *The World and the Parish* (pp. 971–1013).

Arrangement

The order of entries is chronological by date of first publication. Following each title or description is a list of subsequent reprintings of that particular work. When more than one item appeared on the same date (day, month, year), the items are listed alphabetically by newspaper, periodical, or book title. If two or more items appeared in the same publication, they are listed according to page sequence. Entries for which the day of publication is not known are treated as if they appeared on the first day of the month. Entries for which neither the day nor the month of publication is known are treated as if they were published at the first of the year.

The titles of Willa Cather's various newspaper columns seldom afford any clue to the subject or subjects discussed. Therefore, as a guide to the contents of each column, the Checklist borrows the subject listings used by William M. Curtin in the bibliography of *The World and the Parish*. To illustrate: From November 11, 1894, to July 14, 1895, Willa Cather wrote thirty-three columns for the *Nebraska State Journal* under the title "As You Like It." Using the first of these columns as an example, the subject listing indicates that it discusses Olga Nethersole, private libraries, Bliss Carman, Pauline Hall, and the French.

In most cases, references to reprintings in *The Kingdom of Art* and *The World and the Parish* pertain to partial columns, for Slote and Curtin excluded such material as announcements of present or coming theatrical attractions, cast listings, rewrites of press releases, and items picked up from other newspapers or periodicals.

The Appendix lists Willa Cather's known contributions to University of Nebraska campus publications during her student years. Included here are items originally published in the *Hesperian*, at that time a bi-monthly literary magazine, and in the yearbook *Sombrero*. It has been established that Cather also contributed to another student publication, *Lasso*, but as yet no definite attributions have been made. For a fuller discussion, see "University Writing" in *The Kingdom of Art*, pp. 461–62.

It will be apparent from the Introduction that this Checklist owes its existence to the patient and imaginative research of the scholars whose work it compiles. I know that for several the "quest for Cather" has extended over many years. My debt to them is profound.

JoANNA LATHROP

University of Nebraska—Lincoln

WILLA CATHER
A Checklist of Her Published Writing

ABBREVIATIONS

N. B. Check entry under copyright date for complete
citation on books.

Newspapers and Magazines*

HM	Home Monthly (Pittsburgh, Pennsylvania)
IPL	Index of Pittsburg Life
NSJ	Nebraska State Journal (Lincoln)
PG	Pittsburgh Gazette
PL	Pittsburg Leader

[At the turn of the century both forms, Pittsburgh
and Pittsburg, were used; the form followed here is
as the name appeared on the publication.]

Short Story Collections

CSF	Willa Cather's Collected Short Fiction, 1892-1912, 1965.
OD	Obscure Destinies, 1932.
TOB	The Old Beauty and Others, 1948.
TG	The Troll Garden, 1905.
UV	Uncle Valentine and Other Stories: Willa Cather's Uncollected Short Fiction, 1915-1929, 1973.
YBM	Youth and the Bright Medusa, 1920.

Poetry Collections

AT	April Twilights, 1903.
ATOP	April Twilights and Other Poems, 1923.
AT3	April Twilights (1903), 1962.

Other Collections

CY	Writings from Willa Cather's Campus Years,

	1950.
KA	The Kingdom of Art: Willa Cather's First Principles and Critical Statements, 1893-1896, 1966.
NUF	Not Under Forty, 1936.
OW	Willa Cather on Writing: Critical Studies on Writing as an Art, 1949.
W&P	The World and the Parish: Willa Cather's Articles and Reviews, 1893-1902, 1970. 2 vols. numbered consecutively with vol. 2 beginning at p. 503.
WCE	Willa Cather in Europe: Her Own Story of the First Journey, 1956.

Collected Works

Library ed.   The Novels and Stories of Willa
                   Cather, 1937-41.

* The following newspapers and magazines are not
   abbreviated:

Courier (Lincoln, Nebraska)
Library (Pittsburgh, Pennsylvania)
Lincoln Evening News (Nebraska)

1891

Mar. 1 "Concerning Thos. Carlyle." College theme.
Signed W. C. NSJ, p. 14.
KA, pp. 421-25. [Hesperian version is
reprinted; see "Student Writing," same
date.]

Nov. 1 "Shakespeare and Hamlet." First part of
essay. Unsigned. NSJ, p. 16.
KA, pp. 426-32.

8 "Shakespeare and Hamlet." Second part of
essay. Signed W. C. NSJ, p. 11.
KA, pp. 432-36.

1892

May 21 "Peter." Short story. Signed Willa Cather.
Mahogany Tree, pp. 323-24.
Library, 21 July 1900, p. 5. [Retitled
"Peter Sadelack, Father of Anton" and
revised, with additional alterations
from the Hesperian version; see
"Student Writing," 24 November 1892.]
CY, pp. 41-45. [Hesperian version.]
Early Stories. Selected by Mildred R.
Bennett. New York: Dodd, Mead & Co.,
1957, pp. 1-8. [Hesperian and Library
versions.]
CSF, pp. 541-43. [Mahogany Tree version.]

1893

Nov. 5 "One Way of Putting It." Vignettes. Unsigned. NSJ, p. 13.
W&P, pp. 5-7, 10, 25-26.

12 "One Way of Putting It." Vignettes. Unsigned. NSJ, p. 13.
W&P, pp. 9-10, 14-15, 16, 21-22.

[1893]

19 "One Way of Putting It." Vignettes. Unsigned. NSJ, p. 9.
W&P, pp. 17-19, 23, 26-27.

22 "Amusements." Review of Walker Whiteside in
Richelieu. Unsigned. NSJ, p. 6.

23 "Amusements." Review of Clara Morris in
Camille. Unsigned. NSJ, p. 5.
KA, pp. 262-63.
W&P, pp. 43-44.

26 "One Way of Putting It." Vignettes. Unsigned. NSJ, p. 10.
W&P, pp. 10-11, 13-14, 21, 44-45.

30 "Amusements." Review of Robert Downing in
Virginius. Unsigned. NSJ, p. 6.

Dec.   3 "One Way of Putting It." Vignettes, Robert
Downing. Unsigned. NSJ, p. 13.
W&P, pp. 11-13, 15-16, 24-25, 26, 27-28.

14 "Amusements." Review of Friends titled
"'Friends' is Purely Ideal." signed W. C.
NSJ, p. 6.
KA, pp. 263-64.
W&P, pp. 28-29.

17 "One Way of Putting It." Vignettes. Unsigned. NSJ, p. 13.
W&P, pp. 7-9, 16-17, 19-20, 20-21, 29.

1894
Jan. 10 "Amusements." Review of Emily Bancker in
Gloriana. Signed W. C. NSJ, p. 6.
KA, pp. 264-65.

18 "Amusements." Review of Lewis Morrison's

6

[1894]   Faust. Unsigned. NSJ, p. 5.
          W&P, pp. 76-77.

     20   "Amusements." Review of Hoyt's A Trip to
            Chinatown. Unsigned. NSJ, p. 3.

     21   "One Way of Putting It." Comments on the
            theatre. Unsigned. NSJ, p. 16.
            KA, pp. 140, 174-75, 205-206, 207, 256-
            57.

     26   "Amusements." Review of James O'Neill in
            Monte Cristo. Unsigned. NSJ, p. 6.
            KA, p. 139.

     28   "One Way of Putting It." Miscellaneous
            comments. Unsigned. NSJ, p. 13.
            KA, pp. 175-76, 182-83.

Feb. 7   "Amusements." On the Kendals in The Iron-
            master. Unsigned. NSJ, p. 3.
            W&P, pp. 33-35.

      9   "Amusements." Review of The Spider and the
            Fly. Unsigned. NSJ, p. 6.
            KA, pp. 252-53.

     11   "The Critic's Province." Editorial. Unsign-
            ed. NSJ, p. 12.
            W&P, pp. 68-69.

          "Plays and Players." On Lincoln theatre-
            goers, the Kendals, the Gerry Society.
            Signed "Deus Gallery." NSJ, p. 13.
            W&P, pp. 50-51, 84.

     13   "Amusements." Review of Fantasma. Unsigned.
            NSJ, p. 5.

     17   "The Curtain Falls." On the performance of
            Greek and Latin plays at the University

                              7

[1894]   of Nebraska. Unsigned. <u>NSJ</u>, p. 5.
              <u>W&P</u>, pp. 72-74.

    20   "Amusements." Review of <u>A Duel of Hearts</u>
         with Craigen and Paulding. Unsigned.
         <u>NSJ</u>, p. 2.
         <u>KA</u>, pp. 265-67.

    21   "Amusements." Review of one-act plays, <u>The</u>
         <u>Setting Sun</u> and <u>The Dowager Countess</u> with
         Craigen and Paulding. Unsigned. <u>NSJ</u>,
         p. 3.
         <u>KA</u>, p. 267.

    22   "Amusements." Review of <u>In Old Kentucky</u>.
         Unsigned. <u>NSJ</u>, p. 5.

    24   "Amusements." Review of second performance
         of Greek and Latin plays. Unsigned. <u>NSJ</u>,
         p. 6.
         <u>KA</u>, p. 216.

    25   "With Plays and Players." On Greek tragedy,
         Lillian Lewis, Ostrovsky, Modjeska. Un-
         signed. <u>NSJ</u>, p. 9.
         <u>KA</u>, pp. 134-35, 220-21.
         <u>W&P</u>, pp. 37-38, 61-62, 74-75, 96.

Mar.   1   "Amusements." Review of Julia Marlowe in
            <u>The Love Chase</u>. Unsigned. <u>NSJ</u>, p. 3.

        2   "Amusements." Review of <u>The Ensign</u>. Un-
            signed. <u>NSJ</u>, p. 3.

        4   "With Plays and Players." On Julia Mar-
            lowe, Steele MacKaye, Sarah Bernhardt,
            Olive May. Signed "Deus Gallerie." <u>NSJ</u>,
            p. 13.
            <u>CY</u>, pp. 33-34, 35, 35-36.
            <u>W&P</u>, pp. 36-37, 39-40, 41-42.

8

[1894]
11 "With Plays and Players." On Modjeska,
    Maggie Mitchell, Warde, and James, Eng-
    lish taste. Unsigned. NSJ, p. 13.
    CY, pp. 36, 37.
    KA, pp. 199, 221-22, 223, 224.
    W&P, pp. 38, 51, 62-63.

13 "Amusements." Review of Romeo and Juliet
    with Craigen and Paulding. Unsigned.
    NSJ, p. 2.
    W&P, pp. 84-86.

14 "Amusements." Review of A Duel of Hearts
    with Craigen and Paulding. Unsigned. NSJ,
    p. 2.

16 "Amusements." Review of The White Squadron.
    Unsigned. NSJ, p. 3.
    KA, p. 253.

17 "Amusements." Review of The Idea. Unsigned.
    NSJ, p. 3.

22 "Amusements." Review of The Voodoo. Un-
    signed. NSJ, p. 6.
    KA, pp. 251-52.

23 "Amusements." Review of Lewis Morrison in
    Richelieu. Unsigned. NSJ, p. 3.

25 "Between the Acts." On criticism, Clara
    Morris, romance and realism, Lewis
    Morrison. Unsigned. NSJ, p. 13.
    KA, pp. 186-87.
    W&P, pp. 46-49, 77.

30 "Amusements." Review of Herrmann the
    Magician. Unsigned. NSJ, p. 8.

Apr. 1 "Between the Acts." On Lincoln theatres,

9

[1894]   Marie Tempest. Unsigned. NSJ, p. 13.
                [Doubtful; see KA or W&P on their
                tests for authenticity.]

   3 "Amusements." Review of The Black Crook.
      Unsigned. NSJ, p. 5.

   4 "Amusements." Review of Marie Tempest in
      The Fencing Master. Unsigned. NSJ, p. 5.
      W&P, pp. 169-70.

   5 "Amusements." Review of William Crane in
      Brother John. Unsigned. NSJ, p. 6.
      W&P, pp. 78-79.

   6 "Amusements." Review of Police Patrol.
      Unsigned. NSJ, p. 6.

   7 "Amusements." Review of Della Fox and De-
      Wolf Hopper in Panjandrum. Unsigned.
      NSJ, p. 2.
      W&P, pp. 170-71.

   8 "Between the Acts." On plays of the week,
      Cora Tanner, Mounet-Sully, Marie Tempest.
      Unsigned. NSJ, p. 13.
      CY, pp. 37-38.
      KA, pp. 127-28, 215-16.
      W&P, pp. 51, 80-82.

  15 "Between the Acts." On Mrs. Kendal, Gilbert
      and Sullivan, Rider Haggard's She. Un-
      signed. NSJ, p. 13.
      CY, pp. 38-39, 39-40, 40.

  18 "Amusements." Review of a minstrel show.
      Unsigned. NSJ, p. 3.

  20 "Amusements." Review of She. Unsigned.
      NSJ, p. 6.
      KA, pp. 267-68.

22 "Between the Acts." On dramatizing novels, Sousa, Richard Mansfield. Unsigned. <u>NSJ</u>, p. 13.
<u>KA</u>, pp. 209, 253.

24 "Amusements." Review of Richard Mansfield in <u>Beau Brummell</u>. Unsigned. <u>NSJ</u>, p. 5.
<u>KA</u>, pp. 122-23.

26 "Amusements." Review of <u>The District Fair</u>. Unsigned. <u>NSJ</u>, p. 5.

27 "Amusements." Review of vaudeville. Unsigned. <u>NSJ</u>, p. 6.

29 "Between the Acts." On Richard Mansfield, Shakespeare's birthday. Unsigned. <u>NSJ</u>, p. 13.
"Willa Cather on Shakespeare." <u>Prairie Schooner</u> 38 (1964):67-68.
<u>KA</u>, p. 123.
<u>W&P</u>, pp. 54-56, 83-84.

May 4 "Amusements." Review of Salvini in <u>The Three Guardsmen</u>. Unsigned. <u>NSJ</u>, p. 6.
<u>KA</u>, pp. 121-22, 247.

5 "Amusements." Review of Sousa band concert. Unsigned. <u>NSJ</u>, p. 2.
<u>KA</u>, pp. 199-201.

"Amusements." Review of recital by California poet-humorist Fred Emerson Brooks. Unsigned. <u>NSJ</u>, p. 2.

18 "Amusements." Review of Blind Tom, Negro pianist. Unsigned. <u>NSJ</u>, p. 6.
"Willa Cather: A Portfolio." <u>Prairie Schooner</u> 38 (1964):343-44.
<u>W&P</u>, pp. 166-67.

[1894]

27 "Under the White Tents." Feature story on circus. Signed Willa Cather. NSJ, p. 13. W&P, pp. 100-102.

28 "The Competitive Drill." Annual contest of University Cadet Corps. Feature story. Signed Willa Cather. NSJ, p. 13.

June 5 "Amusements." Review of Lady Windermere's Fan. Signed W. C. NSJ, p. 1.
KA, pp. 388-89.
W&P, pp. 90-92.

7 "Amusements." Review of The Chimes of Normandy. Signed W. C. NSJ, p. 2.

July 5 "The Fourth at Crete." Description of the programs on July 3 and 4 including three lectures on modern French art, sculpture, and Dutch and German painters by Lorado Taft. Signed Willa Cather. Lincoln Evening News, p. 8.
"Willa Cather Reports Chautauqua, 1894." Selections in the above article by Bernice Slote. Prairie Schooner 43 (1969):119, 121, 123.

6 "At the Chautauqua." Daily life at the assembly, lectures on "The Roman Empire" by Dr. Joseph T. Duryea and on the "Conscience of the State" by Bayard Holmes. Signed Willa Cather. Lincoln Evening News, p. 1.
"Willa Cather Reports Chautauqua, 1894." Selections in the above article by Bernice Slote. Prairie Schooner 43 (1969):120, 122.

7 "Notable Concert." Lecture by Professor L. Fossler on Teutonic religion, song

[1894]   recital by Miss Electra Gifford. Signed Willa Cather. Lincoln <u>Evening</u> <u>News</u>, p. 5.
"Willa Cather Reports Chautauqua, 1894."
    Selections in the above article by Bernice Slote. <u>Prairie</u> <u>Schooner</u> 43 (1969):119, 123-24.

9   "Sunday at Crete." Description of a Chautauqua dinner, lecture on Biblical criticism by Professor Charles F. Kent. Signed Willa Cather. Lincoln <u>Evening</u> <u>News</u>, p. 5.
"Willa Cather Reports Chautauqua, 1894."
    Selections in the above article by Bernice Slote. <u>Prairie</u> <u>Schooner</u> 43 (1969):120-21, 122.

10   Life at Crete." Piano recital by Mrs. Will Owen Jones. Signed Willa Cather. Lincoln <u>Evening</u> <u>News</u>, p. 4.
"Willa Cather Reports Chautauqua, 1894."
    Selections in the above article by Bernice Slote. <u>Prairie</u> <u>Schooner</u> 43 (1969):120, 124-25.

11   "In Dunning Hall." Description of the dormitory for the staff and performers, song recital by Mrs. Katherine Fisk. Signed Willa Cather. Lincoln <u>Evening</u> <u>News</u>, p. 5.
"Willa Cather Reports Chautauqua, 1894."
    Selections in the above article by Bernice Slote. <u>Prairie</u> <u>Schooner</u> 43 (1969):126.

12   "Crete Chautauqua." Anne L. Barr's class in physical education, dramatic impersonations by Charles F. Underwood, song recital by Mrs. Fisk. Signed Willa Cather. Lincoln <u>Evening</u> <u>News</u>, p. 4.
"Willa Cather Reports Chautauqua, 1894."
    Selections in the above article by

13

[1894]   Bernice Slote. _Prairie Schooner_ 43
                (1969):125.

     13   "Mrs. Fisk's Concert." Awarding of diplomas
          to Chautauqua graduates, lectures by Dr.
          Duryea and Prof. Holmes, concert by Mrs.
          Fisk and mixed chorus. Signed Willa
          Cather. Lincoln _Evening News_, p. 5.

     14   "Empty Cottages." The scene after the as-
          sembly has dispersed. Signed Willa
          Cather. Lincoln _Evening News_, p. 1.
          "Willa Cather Reports Chautauqua, 1894."
            Selections in the above article by
            Bernice Slote. _Prairie Schooner_ 43
            (1969):126-27.

Aug. 12   "An Old River Metropolis." Brownville,
          Nebraska. Feature story. Signed Willa
          Cather. _NSJ_, p. 13.
          American Heritage 21 (October 1970):68-
            72. [Omits last two paragraphs.]
          _W&P_, pp. 103-112.

     29   "Amusements." Review of Cora Potter and
          Kyrle Bellew in _In Society_. Unsigned.
          NSJ, p. 6. [Doubtful; see _KA_ on tests
          for authenticity.]

Sept. 13   "Amusements." Review of Roland Reed in _The
          Woman Hater_. Unsigned. _NSJ_, p. 5.

     14   "Amusements." Review of Royal Entertainers
          in vaudeville. Unsigned. _NSJ_, p. 6.

     16   "Amusements." Review of _Underground_. Un-
          signed. _NSJ_, p. 3.

          "Utterly Irrelevant." On art exhibits at
          the State Fair, interview with a magi-
          cian, _Trilby_. Unsigned. _NSJ_, p. 13.

[1894]   KA, pp. 183, 362.

23 "Utterly Irrelevant." On the use of librar-
    ies, Annie Kenwick, Marion Manola, Sarah
    Grand's The Superfluous Woman, the duty
    of an author. Unsigned. NSJ, p. 13.
    KA, pp. 180-81, 406-407.

28 "Amusements." Review of The Devil's
    Auction. Unsigned. NSJ, p. 3.

30 "Amusements." Review of Uncle Tom's Cabin.
    Unsigned. NSJ, p. 2.
    KA, pp. 269-70.
    Horizon 9 (spring 1967):118.

    "Utterly Irrelevant." On music and theatre.
    Unsigned. NSJ, p. 13.
    KA, pp. 216-17.

Oct. 2 "Amusements." Review of Robert Downing in
    The Gladiator. Unsigned. NSJ, p. 3.
    KA, pp. 270-72.

    5 "Amusements." Review of The Derby Winner.
    Unsigned. NSJ, p. 6.

    7 "Utterly Irrelevant." On William McKinley,
    Robert Downing, church music, theatre
    notes. Unsigned. NSJ, p. 13.
    KA, pp. 177-78.
    W&P, pp. 117-18.

    9 "Amusements." Review of Gloriana. Unsigned.
    NSJ, p. 2.

    12 "Amusements." Review of Charley's Aunt. Un-
    signed. NSJ, p. 5.

    14 "Amusements." Review of Rush City. Unsign-
    ed. NSJ, p. 6.

[1894]

14 "Utterly Irrelevant." On Duse and Bern-
hardt, town and gown, Oliver Wendell
Holmes, war in China, practical educa-
tion. Unsigned. _NSJ_, p. 13.
_KA_, pp. 117-18.
_W&P_, pp. 112-14, 114-15, 129-30.

20 "Under the Golden Leaves of Autumn." A
wedding. Unsigned. _NSJ_, p. 6.

21 "Utterly Irrelevant." On the Lincoln con-
cert season, Queen Victoria, the artist's
role, standards of criticism. Unsigned.
NSJ, p. 13.
_KA_, pp. 141-42, 176-77, 253, 257-58.
_W&P_, pp. 52, 70-71.

25 "Amusements." Review of _The Hustler_. Unsigned. _NSJ_, p. 2.

28 "Utterly Irrelevant." On _Trilby_, theatre
audiences, Sordello Clubs, interview
with an actor in the penitentiary. Unsigned. _NSJ_, p. 13.
_KA_, pp. 142-43, 179-80, 184-85.
_W&P_, pp. 115-16, 131-32.

30 "Amusements." Review of _A Wife's Honor_.
Unsigned. _NSJ_, p. 2.

31 "Amusements." Review of _Married for Money_.
Unsigned. _NSJ_, p. 6.

Nov. 1 "Music and Drama." Review of Hoyt's _A Trip
to Chinatown_. Unsigned. _NSJ_, p. 2.
_KA_, pp. 241-42.

4 "More or Less Personal." On Hoyt, _The Green
Carnation_, Bacon and Shakespeare, Duse.
Unsigned. _NSJ_, p. 12.

16

[1894]   "Willa Cather on Shakespeare." <u>Prairie</u>
                    <u>Schooner</u> 38 (1964):68-71.
                <u>KA</u>, pp. 135-36, 152-53, 242.
                <u>W&P</u>, pp. 56-57, 86-89.

     6   "Amusements." Review of Royle's <u>Friends</u>.
            Unsigned. <u>NSJ</u>, p. 8.
            <u>KA</u>, pp. 272-73.

     7   "Amusements." Review of <u>Hot Tamales</u>. Un-
            signed. <u>NSJ</u>, p. 5.

     9   "Amusements." Review of <u>Oh, What a Night</u>.
            Unsigned. <u>NSJ</u>, p. 6.

    10   "Amusements." Review of <u>Pinafore</u>. Unsigned.
            <u>NSJ</u>, p. 6.

    11   "As You Like It." On Olga Nethersole, pri-
            vate libraries, Bliss Carman, Pauline
            Hall, the French. Unsigned. <u>NSJ</u>, p. 13.
            <u>KA</u>, pp. 137, 181, 224.
            <u>W&P</u>, pp. 58-59, 116, 119-20, 134-35.

    14   "Music and Drama." Review of "Gustave
            Frohman's Company No. 13" in <u>Jane</u> and
            <u>The Great Mogul</u>. Unsigned. <u>NSJ</u>, p. 2.

    18   "As You Like It." On criticism, Mrs. Ken-
            dal, Lillie Langtry, Bernhardt. Unsigned.
            <u>NSJ</u>, p. 13.
            <u>KA</u>, pp. 172, 258-59.
            <u>W&P</u>, pp. 40-41, 63-65, 93-95.

    21   "Amusements." Review of Pauline Hall in
            <u>Dorcas</u>. Unsigned. <u>NSJ</u>, p. 2.

    22   "Amusements." Review of the Wilber Enter-
            tainment Company. Unsigned. <u>NSJ</u>, p. 6.

    25   "As You Like It." On Pauline Hall and other

[1894]   operetta stars, death of Anton Rubin-
                stein. Unsigned. NSJ, p. 13.
                KA, pp. 134, 228-29.
                W&P, pp. 65-66, 121, 167-69, 172-74.

Dec.   2   "As You Like It." On football, stage
                marriages, Robert B. Mantell, and
                Maurice Barrymore. Unsigned. NSJ, p. 13.
                KA, pp. 151-52, 212-13.

        4   "Amusements." Review of Nat Goodwin in
                A Gilded Fool. Unsigned. NSJ, p. 8.
                KA, pp. 128-29.

        5   "Music and Drama." Review of A Summer
                Blizzard. Unsigned. NSJ, p. 3.
                KA, p. 252.

        8   "Amusements." Review of Killarney. Un-
                signed. NSJ, p. 2.

        9   "Amusements." Review of the Tavary Grand
                Opera Company in Il Trovatore. Unsigned.
                NSJ, p. 4.
                KA, pp. 131-32.

            "As You Like It." On the art of Nat Good-
                win, William Crane in Brother John,
                Lillian Russell, living pictures. Un-
                signed. NSJ, p. 13.
                KA, pp. 129-30, 229.
                W&P, pp. 59-60, 79-80, 121.

        10 "Amusements." Review of Helena von Doen-
                hoff in Il Trovatore. Unsigned. NSJ,
                p. 8.
                KA, p. 132.

        14 "Amusements." Review of Thomas Q. Seabrooke
                in Isle of Champagne. Unsigned. NSJ,
                p. 6.

                            18

15 "Amusements." Review of O'Neil, Washington, D. C. Unsigned. NSJ, p. 2.
KA, pp. 250-51.

16 "As You Like It." On playing Shakespearean
comedy, stage realism, the artist's
social role, Helena von Doenhoff. Unsigned. NSJ, p. 13.
KA, p. 132.
W&P, pp. 52-54, 96-97, 122-23.

18 "Amusements." Review of Lady Windermere's
Fan. Unsigned. NSJ, p. 2.
W&P, p. 92.

20 "Amusements." Review of In Old Kentucky.
Unsigned. NSJ, p. 3.

23 "As You Like It." On Stevenson, Kipling,
Trilby. Unsigned. NSJ, p. 13.
KA, pp. 311-13, 316-18, 363-65.
W&P, pp. 132-34, 135-39.

30 "As You Like It." On Zola and Bernhardt.
Unsigned. NSJ, p. 13.
KA, pp. 116-17.
W&P, pp. 139-42.

1895
Jan.   4 "Amusements." Review of Sol Smith Russell
in The Heir at Law. Unsigned. NSJ, p. 6.

6 "Amusements." Review of Belasco's The
Charity Ball. Unsigned. NSJ, p. 6.
KA, p. 237.
W&P, p. 220.

"As You Like It." On the exhibition of the
Haydon Art Club, Belasco, criticism. Un-

19

[1895]   signed. NSJ, p. 13.
              KA, pp. 217-19.
              W&P, pp. 124-27, 233-34.

     8 "Amusements." Review of Thro' the War. Un-
        signed. NSJ, p. 2.

    11 "Amusements." Review of A Jolly Good Fel-
        low. Unsigned. NSJ, p. 8.
        KA, p. 252.

    12 "Amusements." Review of Yon Yonson. Un-
        signed. NSJ, p. 6.
        KA, p. 273.

    13 "As You Like It." On Sappho, Elizabeth
        Barrett Browning, and Christina Rossetti.
        Unsigned. NSJ, p. 13.
        KA, pp. 346-49, 349.
        W&P, pp. 143-47.

    18 "Amusements." Review of Warde and James in
        Henry IV. Unsigned. NSJ, p. 8.
        KA, pp. 288-90.

    20 "As You Like It." On Shakespeare's history
        plays, Julia Marlowe. Unsigned. NSJ,
        p. 13.
        "Willa Cather on Shakespeare." Prairie
           Schooner 38 (1964):71-73.
        KA, pp. 290-91.
        W&P, pp. 230-31.

    22 "Amusements." Review of Belasco's Men and
        Women. Unsigned. NSJ, p. 8.
        KA, pp. 237-38.

    23 "Amusements." Review of recital by elocu-
        tionist and violinist. Unsigned. NSJ,
        p. 6.

[1895]

26 "Amusements." Review of J. K. Emmett in
Fritz in a Madhouse. Unsigned. NSJ,
p. 6.
KA, pp. 139-40.

27 "Amusements." Review of Belasco's The Girl
I Left Behind Me. Unsigned. NSJ, p. 6.

"As You Like It." On Belasco's plays,
interview with Bernice Wheeler, marriage
of Helena von Doenhoff, Dumas fils, Nat
Goodwin. Unsigned. NSJ, p. 13.
KA, pp. 238-40, 247-48.
W&P, pp. 175-76, 220-22, 222-23.

Feb.   1 "Amusements." Review of Hendrick Hudson.
Unsigned. NSJ, p. 5.

2 "Amusements." Review of Charley's Aunt.
Unsigned. NSJ, p. 6.

3 "As You Like It." Interview with Gustave
Frohman. Unsigned. NSJ, p. 13.
W&P, pp. 224-28.

7 "Amusements." Review of Hoyt's Temperance
Town. Unsigned. NSJ, p. 6.

10 "As You Like It." On a Mendelssohn concert, Charles Hoyt and American comedy,
the Russian ballerina Ksheninka. Unsigned. NSJ, p. 13.
KA, pp. 242-43.
W&P, pp. 177-78, 234.

14 "Amusements." Review of The Passport. Unsigned. NSJ, p. 2.

17 "As You Like It." On Francois Coppée. Unsigned. NSJ, p. 9.

21

[1895]   KA, pp. 326-27.
              W&P, pp. 147-49.

       22 "Amusements." Review of Eddie Foy in Off
              the Earth. Unsigned. NSJ, p. 8.

       24 "As You Like It." On Browning as a play-
              wright, Max O'Rell lecture, Katherine
              Kidder as Madame San Gêne. Unsigned.
              NSJ, p. 13.
              KA, pp. 137-38, 150-51.
              W&P, pp. 188-90, 204-205.

       26 "Amusements." Review of The New "Paul
              Kauvar" by Steele MacKaye. Unsigned.
              NSJ, p. 6.

Mar.   2 "Amusements." Review of Clay Clement in
              The New Dominion. Unsigned. NSJ, p. 6.
              KA, pp. 124-25.

        3 "Amusements." Review of Tempest in The
              Fencing Master. Unsigned. NSJ, p. 8.
              KA, p. 137.

           "As You Like It." On Dorothy Morton, Clay
              Clement. Unsigned. NSJ, p. 13.
              KA, p. 124.

       10 "As You Like It." On Clay Clement,
              Modjeska, Hamlet, Mrs. James Potter.
              Unsigned. NSJ, p. 13.
              KA, pp. 144-45.
              W&P, pp. 190-93, 194-95, 231-32.

       31 "As You Like It." On Falstaff, Emma Eames
              in Otello. Unsigned. NSJ, p. 13.
              KA, pp. 214-15.
              W&P, pp. 178-82.

Apr.   2 "Amusements." Review of Griffith's

                              22

Faust. Unsigned. NSJ, p. 8.

7 "As You Like It." On the dramatization
of Trilby, actors' private lives. Unsigned. NSJ, p. 13.
KA, p. 133.
W&P, pp. 193-94, 240-41.

14 "As You Like It." On a play called
Nebraska, Beerbohm Tree, Hamlin Garland.
Unsigned. NSJ, p. 13.
KA, pp. 223-24.
W&P, p. 198.

17 "Amusements." Review of Bronson Howard's
Shenandoah. Unsigned. NSJ, p. 5.
KA, pp. 253-54.
W&P, pp. 228-29.

18 "Amusements." Review of The Black Crook.
Unsigned. NSJ, p. 3.
KA, pp. 274-75.

21 "As You Like It." On Shakespeare, Sardou,
Madame Réjane. Unsigned. NSJ, p. 13.
"Willa Cather on Shakespeare." Prairie
Schooner 38 (1964):73-74.
KA, pp. 286-88.
Horizon 9 (spring 1967):117-18.
W&P, pp. 199-200, 232-33, 234-35.

23 "Amusements." Review of the Spooners in
Inez. Unsigned. NSJ, p. 5.
KA, pp. 275-77.

25 "Amusements." Review of Effie Ellsler in
Doris. Unsigned. NSJ, p. 8.
KA, p. 139.

26 "Amusements." Review of the Spooners in

[1895]   The Buckeye. Unsigned. NSJ, p. 8.

    28 "As You Like It." On Marie Wainwright in
         The Daughters of Eve, John L. Sullivan,
         Lillian Russell. Unsigned. NSJ, p. 14.
         KA, pp. 230-31.

May   5 "As You Like It." On Bernhardt, Salvini,
         Max O'Rell and Mark Twain. Unsigned. NSJ,
         p. 14.
         W&P, pp. 150-51.

    12 "As You Like It." On Clara Morris and other
         stars, Julia Magruder's serial Princess
         Sonia. Unsigned. NSJ, p. 12.
         W&P, pp. 152-53, 196, 216-17.

    14 "Amusements." Review of Emily Bancker in
         Our Flat. Unsigned. NSJ, p. 6.

    19 "As You Like It." On Lillian Russell, Ada
         Rehan, Nethersole, Lady Windermere's Fan.
         Unsigned. NSJ, p. 12.
         KA, pp. 208, 389-90.
         W&P, pp. 153-54.

    26 "As You Like It." On Marie Tempest, Chicago
         Chap-Book, Hobart Chatfield-Taylor. Un-
         signed. NSJ, p. 12.
         KA, pp. 224-25.
         W&P, pp. 155-57.

June   2 "As You Like It." On the Trilby fad, Warde
         and James in Henry IV, Sardou. Unsigned.
         NSJ, p. 9.
         W&P, pp. 118, 205.

     7 "Amusements." Review of Oriole Opera Com-
         pany. Unsigned. NSJ, p. 6.

     9 "As You Like It." On Princess Sonia, Melba,

[1895]   theatre notes. Unsigned. NSJ, p. 12.
KA, p. 132.

16 "As You Like It." On Marie Burroughs, Duse,
French taste. Unsigned. NSJ, p. 12.
KA, pp. 118-19, 153-54, 260-61.
W&P, pp. 195, 207-209, 235.

30 "As You Like It." On Henry Irving, Beerbohm Tree, Rubinstein, Max O'Rell, French
and American women. Unsigned. NSJ, p. 12.
KA, pp. 160-61, 189-91.

July 7 "As You Like It." On William Winter as
critic, Lillian Russell, Otis Skinner,
Katherine Fisk. Unsigned. NSJ, p. 9.
W&P, p. 198.

14 "As You Like It." On When Dreams Come True
by Edgar Saltus, William Dean Howells,
Bernhardt's book. Unsigned. NSJ, p. 9.
W&P, pp. 198-99, 259-60, 260-61.

21 "The Passing Show." On Dumas fils, Bern-
hardt, Zola, Mary Anderson, Augustin
Daly, Clara Morris. Unsigned. NSJ, p. 9.
KA, pp. 155, 181.
W&P, pp. 196-97, 200-202, 224.

Aug. 4 "The Passing Show." On Henry Guy Carleton
and Belasco, Olive May interview,
Howells, Henry James, Browning. Unsigned.
NSJ, p. 9.
KA, pp. 243-46.
W&P, pp. 203-204, 237-39.

11 "The Passing Show." On death of Madame
Carvalho, Melba, America and Rome,
Marlowe in Henry IV, Stanley Weyman.
NSJ, p. 9.
KA, pp. 161-62, 195, 216, 323.

25

[1895]   W&P, pp. 182-84, 184-85, 205-206.

24 "The Passing Show." On Patti, Jean de
Reszke and Calvé, Mansfield and Shaw,
the third act of Hamlet, DeWolf Hopper,
Trilby, the opening of the Creighton
Theatre in Omaha. Unsigned. Courier,
pp. 6-8.
KA, pp. 254-55.

31 "The Passing Show." On Felix Morris and
Eddie Foy, Rubinstein's son, Royle's
Mexico, the Bowery as home of talent.
Unsigned. Courier, pp. 6-8.
KA, pp. 195-97.
W&P, pp. 235-36.

Sept. 3 "Amusements." Review of exhibition of
hypnotism. Unsigned. NSJ, p. 6.

5 "Amusements." Review of Roland Reed in
The Politician. Unsigned. NSJ, p. 2.

7 "The Passing Show." On Julia Arthur and
the training of actors, dramatizing
Romola, Ella Wheeler Wilcox, Calvé,
Mascagni. Unsigned. Courier, pp. 6-7.
KA, pp. 162-63, 201, 209-210.
W&P, pp. 210-11, 241.

"The Theatres." Review of Roland Reed in
The Politician, the Flints' hypnotism
act. Unsigned. Courier, p. 8.
KA, pp. 277-78.

10 "Amusements." Review of the Spooners in
The Buckeye. Unsigned. NSJ, p. 8.

11 "Amusements." Review of Griffith's Faust.
Unsigned. NSJ, p. 8.
KA, pp. 279-80.

26

14 "The Passing Show." On George Sand's Con-
   suelo, Kipling and Anthony Hope Hawkins,
   the Dovey sisters. Unsigned. Courier,
   pp. 6-7.
   KA, pp. 146-47, 210, 318-21.

   "The Theatres." Review of Griffith's Faust,
   the Spooners. Unsigned. Courier, p. 8.
   KA, pp. 280-81.

21 "The Passing Show." On Hall Caine, Duse
   Sir Henry Irving, Marion Crawford. Un-
   signed. Courier, pp. 6-7.
   KA, pp. 119, 329.
   W&P, pp. 209-210, 211-12, 261-62

24 "Amusements." Review of The Hustler. Unsigned. NSJ, p. 8.

25 "Amusements." Review of Belasco's The Wife.
   Unsigned. NSJ, p. 3.

27 "Amusements." Review of Rush City. Unsigned. NSJ, p. 8.

28 "The Passing Show." On Oscar Wilde, Judith
   Gautier, Zélie de Lussan, Clara Morris.
   Unsigned. Courier, pp. 6-7.
   KA, pp. 133, 138-39, 390-93.
   W&P, pp. 263-66.

   "The Theatres." Review of Belasco's The
   Wife. Unsigned. Courier, p. 8.
   KA, pp. 281-82.

   "Man and Woman/A Symposium." Contribution.
   Signed Willa Cather. Courier, p. 10.
   W&P, p. 127.

Oct. 2 "Amusements." Review of William Gillette in

[1895]   Too Much Johnson. Unsigned. NSJ, p. 3.

    5 "The Passing Show." On Nell Gwyn, Maude
       Adams and Richard Harding Davis, Howells
       and Harper's, Paganini. Unsigned.
       Courier, pp. 6-7.
       KA, pp. 164-65, 358-59.
       W&P, pp. 266-67.

       "The Theatres." Review of William Gillette
       in Too Much Johnson. Unsigned. Courier,
       p. 8.

   10 "Amusements." Review of Hoyt's A Contented
       Woman. Unsigned. NSJ, p. 5.
       KA, p. 243.

   12 "The Passing Show." On Poe. Unsigned.
       Courier, pp. 6-7.
       KA, pp. 380-87.
       W&P, pp. 157-63.

   15 "Amusements." Review of Human Hearts. Un-
       signed. NSJ, p. 6.

   17 "Amusements." Review of the Dovey Sisters.
       Unsigned. NSJ, p. 2.
       KA, p. 148.

   19 "The Passing Show." On Richard Harding
       Davis and Anne Reeve Aldrich, Amélie
       Rives Chandler, Margaret Mather, Cora
       Potter. Unsigned. Courier, pp. 6-7.
       W&P, pp. 213-14.

   23 "Amusements." Review of Lillian Lewis in
       Cleopatra. Unsigned. NSJ, p. 6.
       KA, pp. 292-93.
       Horizon 9 (Spring 1967):116-17.

   25 "Amusements." Review of DeWolf Hopper in

                           28

[1895]   <u>Wang</u>. Unsigned. <u>NSJ</u>, p. 6.
              <u>KA</u>, p. 140.

        26 "The Passing Show." On Lillian Lewis as
            Cleopatra, Josef Hofmann. Unsigned.
            <u>Courier</u>, pp. 6-7.
            <u>KA</u>, pp. 148-49, 293-97.
            <u>Horizon</u> 9 (Spring 1967):117.
            <u>W&P</u>, pp. 185-86, 242-46.

        30 "Amusements." Review of <u>The Globe Trotter</u>.
            Unsigned. <u>NSJ</u>, p. 6.

        31 "Amusements." Review of <u>The Black Crook</u>.
            Unsigned. <u>NSJ</u>, p. 2.
            <u>KA</u>, p. 275.

Nov.   2   "The Passing Show." On DeWolf Hopper, Ro-
            mance, Stevenson's letters, Nat Goodwin.
            Unsigned. <u>Courier</u>, pp. 6-7.
            <u>KA</u>, pp. 130-31, 231-33, 313-14.
            <u>W&P</u>, pp. 214-16, 268-70, 271.

            "The Theatres." Reviews of Mrs. Dion Bouci-
            cault in <u>The Globe Trotter</u>, <u>The Black
            Crook</u>. Unsigned. <u>Courier</u>, p. 8.

        7   "Amusements." Review of <u>The Colonel's
            Wives</u>. Unsigned. <u>NSJ</u>, p. 3.

        9   "The Passing Show." On Anthony Hope's Zenda
            stories, Pierre Loti's <u>The Romance of a
            Spahi</u>, Dumas' <u>Route de Thèbes</u>, death of
            Eugene Field, <u>The Colonel's Wives</u>. Un-
            signed. <u>Courier</u>, pp. 6-7.
            <u>KA</u>, pp. 215, 321, 332, 365-67.
            <u>W&P</u>, p. 272.

        16 "The Passing Show." On overproductive writ-
            ers, James. Unsigned. <u>Courier</u>, pp. 6-7.
            <u>KA</u>, pp. 222-23, 360-61.

                        29

[1895]   W&P, pp. 273-75.

21 "Amusements." Review of Walker Whiteside in
      Hamlet. Unsigned. NSJ, p. 6.
      KA, pp. 304-305.
      W&P, pp. 247-48.

23 "The Passing Show." On Ouida and women
      novelists, Walker Whiteside's Hamlet.
      Unsigned. Courier, pp. 7-8.
      KA, pp. 305-308, 408-409.
      W&P, pp. 248-51, 275-77.

24 "Amusements." Review of Robert Downing in
      Sardou's Helena. Unsigned. NSJ, p. 3.

26 "Amusements." Review of Emily Bancker in
      Our Flat. Unsigned. NSJ, p. 6.

30 "The Passing Show." On Swinburne, Scottish
      writers--Ian Maclaren, Samuel Crockett,
      James M. Barrie. Unsigned. Courier,
      pp. 6-7.
      KA, pp. 338-41, 349-50.
      W&P, pp. 277-79.

Dec. 6 "Amusements." Review of Effie Ellsler in
      As You Like It. Unsigned. NSJ, p. 6.
      KA, p. 298.
      Horizon 9 (Spring 1967):118-19.

13 "Amusements." Review of Newest Devil's
      Auction. Unsigned. NSJ, p. 3.

14 "Amusements." Review of Louis James in
      Othello. Unsigned. NSJ, p. 6.
      KA, pp. 299-300.
      W&P, pp. 252-53.

15 "The Passing Show." On Dumas fils, Pade-
      rewski, Heine, the Intermezzo from

[1895]   *Cavalleria Rusticana*. Unsigned. NSJ,
              p. 9.
              KA, pp. 183-84, 204, 248-49.

       22   "The Passing Show." On Louis James as
              Othello, Mansfield, a charity concert.
              Unsigned. NSJ, p. 9.
              KA, pp. 202, 300-302.
              W&P, pp. 253-54.

1896
Jan.   "On the Divide." Short Story. Signed W.
              Cather. Overland Monthly, Ser. 2, 27:
              65-74.
              Early Stories. Selected by Mildred R.
                 Bennett. New York: Dodd, Mead & Co.,
                 1957, pp. 59-75.
              CSF, pp. 493-504.

        5   "The Passing Show." On Stevenson's letters,
              Victor Maurel, Calvé, Clay Clement. Un-
              signed. NSJ, p. 9.
              KA, pp. 214, 314-16.

       12   "The Passing Show." On Hall Caine's The
              Bondman, Campanini, the divorce of Sadie
              Martinot, Ladies' Home Journal. Unsigned.
              NSJ, p. 9.
              KA, pp. 165-66, 187-89, 329-30.

       19   "The Passing Show." On Yvette Guilbert,
              Alfred Austin as Poet Laureate, monument
              to Stevenson, Lillie Langtry, Walt Whit-
              man. Unsigned. NSJ, p. 9.
              KA, pp. 166-67, 192, 225-28, 351-53.
              Horizon 9 (Spring 1967):119.
              W&P, pp. 280-82.

       26   "The Passing Show." On James Lane Allen,
              Bernhardt, death of Pearl Etynge. Un-

[1896]   signed. <u>NSJ</u>, p. 9.
                    <u>KA</u>, pp. <u>1</u>20-21, 330-31.

        31 "Amusements." Review of <u>Wang</u> with Albert
            Hart. Unsigned. <u>NSJ</u>, p. <u>6</u>.

Feb.   2 "The Passing Show." On the death of Paul
            Verlaine, Thomas Hardy's <u>Jude the</u>
            <u>Obscure</u>. Unsigned. <u>NSJ</u>, p. <u>9</u>.
            <u>KA</u>, pp. 359-60, 393-<u>97</u>.
            <u>W&P</u>, pp. 282-86.

         4 "Amusements." Review of the Holdens in
            <u>Roxy</u>, <u>the Waif</u>. Unsigned. <u>NSJ</u>, p. 6.

         9 "The Passing Show." On the English Poet
            Laureate, Dumas <u>fils</u>, Robert W. Inger-
            soll. Unsigned. <u>NSJ</u>, p. 9.
            <u>KA</u>, pp. 192-93, <u>2</u>10-11, 225, 249.

      16 "The Passing Show." On Zola's <u>The Fat and</u>
            <u>the Thin</u>, Bernhardt, Margaret Mather.
            Unsigned. <u>NSJ</u>, p. 9.
            <u>KA</u>, pp. 36<u>8</u>-71.

      23 "The Passing Show." On Eugene Field's <u>The</u>
            <u>Love Affairs of a Bibliomaniac</u>, Oscar
            Hammerstein, Marie Corelli. Unsigned.
            <u>NSJ</u>, p. 9.
            <u>KA</u>, pp. 193-94, 202-203, 208-209, 254,
             332-33.

Mar. 1 "The Passing Show." On <u>Mary Magdalen</u> by
            Edgar Saltus, Richard Hovey, Ambroise
            Thomas and Père-Lachaise, Duse-Bernhardt
            duel. Unsigned. <u>NSJ</u>, p. 9.
            <u>KA</u>, pp. 167-68, 35<u>4</u>-56, 415-17.

        8 "The Passing Show." On Byron, Herbert
            Bates, Amélie Rives, summary of theatre
            season. Unsigned. <u>NSJ</u>, p. 13.

[1896] KA, pp. 203-204, 334-35, 398-99.
W&P, pp. 254-55.

15 "The Passing Show." On Conan Doyle, Dumas père, prodigies, Max Nordau, Anatole France. Unsigned. NSJ, p. 9.
KA, pp. 324-25, 327-28.

22 "The Passing Show." On Herbert Bates, the realism of Anna Karenina, mystery stories and Stevenson's The Wrecker, Duse. Unsigned. NSJ, p. 9.
KA, pp. 154, 193, 335-36, 378-79.
W&P, pp. 287-88.

26 "Amusements." Review of Fleur de Lis. Unsigned. NSJ, p. 2.
KA, pp. 283-84.

29 "Amusements." Review of Richard Mansfield in A Parisian Romance. Unsigned. NSJ, p. 5.
KA, pp. 284-85.
W&P, pp. 217-18.

"The Passing Show." On Henry James's The Tragic Muse as a novel of the stage, Sol Smith Russell in Mr. Valentine's Christmas and An Everyday Man. Unsigned. NSJ, p. 9.
KA, pp. 361-62.
W&P, pp. 288-89.

Apr. 5 "The Passing Show." On Henri Murger's Scènes de la vie de Bohème, death of Jennie Kimball. Unsigned. NSJ, p. 16.
KA, pp. 410-14.
W&P, pp. 292-96.

12 "The Passing Show." On The Crime of Sylvestre Bonnard, Tom Brown's Schooldays,

33

[1896]   Mansfield, Minnie Maddern Fiske. Unsigned. NSJ, p. 13.
KA, pp. 328-29, 336-38.

19 "The Passing Show." On Anthony Hope's
Phroso, Bernice Harraden, the Chicago
Chap-Book, Sir Richard and Lady Burton,
and the author of "Kathleen Mavourneen."
Unsigned. NSJ, p. 13.
KA, pp. 168-69, 185-86, 322.
W&P, pp. 289-90.

26 "The Passing Show." On Hovey and Carman,
Bernhardt, Lillian Russell. Unsigned.
NSJ, p. 13.
KA, pp. 353-54.
W&P, pp. 290-91.

May   3 "The Passing Show." On Mary Anderson, Pade-
rewski's prize for American composers.
Unsigned. NSJ, p. 13.
KA, pp. 155-59.
W&P, p. 202.

10 "The Passing Show." On The Rivals, prolific
authors, notes on stars. Unsigned. NSJ,
p. 13.
W&P, pp. 262-63.

17 "The Passing Show." On Ruskin, Tolstoi's
new art. Unsigned. NSJ, p. 13.
KA, pp. 378, 400-404.
W&P, pp. 291-92, 297-301.

24 "The Passing Show." On Burns and Scottish
writers, Kipling and the Balestiers. Unsigned. NSJ, p. 13.
KA, pp. 341-44.

31 "The Passing Show." On Mrs. Humphry Ward
and George Eliot, Nethersole and Daly,

[1896] Henry Irving's stagecraft. Unsigned.
        NSJ, p. 13.
        KA, pp. 216, 375-77.

June   "A Night at Greenway Court." Short story.
        Signed Willa Cather. Nebraska Literary
        Magazine 1:215-24.
        Library, 21 April 1900, pp. 5-7. [Re-
          vised version.]
        CY, pp. 80-92. [Nebraska Literary ver-
          sion.]
        Early Stories. Selected by Mildred R.
          Bennett. New York: Dodd, Mead & Co.,
          1957, pp. 77-91. [Both versions.]
        CSF, pp. 483-92. [Nebraska Literary
          version.]

    7   "The Passing Show." On a personal letter
        from Clay Clement, Daudet and the roman
        à clef. NSJ, p. 13.

   12   "Amusements." Review of Boston Comic Opera
        Company in Olivette. Unsigned. NSJ, p. 6.

   14   "The Passing Show." On Frances Hodgson Bur-
        nett's A Lady of Quality, the failure of
        Abbey and Grau, death of Clara Wieck
        Schumann. Unsigned. NSJ, p. 13.
        KA, pp. 169-70, 197-98, 372-74.

Aug.   "Tommy, the Unsentimental." Short story.
        Signed Willa Cather. HM 6:6-7.
        Early Stories. Selected by Mildred R.
          Bennett. New York: Dodd, Mead & Co.,
          1957, pp. 103-113.
        CSF, pp. 473-80.

        "La Pucelle Again." Editorial. Unsigned.
        HM 6:12.

        "The Princess Baladina--Her Adventure."

35

[1896]   Short story. Signed "Charles Douglass."
              HM 6:20-21.
              CSF, pp. 567-72.

              "My Little Boy." Poem. Signed "John Esten."
              HM 6:21.
              AT3. Rev. ed., pp. 64-65.

Sept.   "Stevenson's Monument." Article. Unsigned.
              HM 6:3.

              "Two Women the World is Watching." Article
              on Mrs. William McKinley and Mrs. William
              Jennings Bryan. Signed "Mary K. Hawley."
              HM 6:4-5.
              Library, 14 July 1900, pp. 13-15. [Parts
                included in an article, "The Personal
                Side of William Jennings Bryan."]
              W&P, pp. 309-313.

              "The Count of Crow's Nest." Short story.
              Signed Willa Cather. HM 6:9-11. [Con-
              cluded in HM 6 (October 1896):12-13, 22-
              23.]
              Early Stories. Selected by Mildred R.
                Bennett. New York: Dodd, Mead & Co.,
                1957, pp. 115-45.
              CSF, pp. 449-71.

              "The Burns Centenary." Editorial. Unsigned.
              HM 6:12.
              W&P, p. 314.

      22 Review of Roland Reed in The Wrong Mr.
              Wright. Unsigned. PL, p. 9.

Oct.   "The Count of Crow's Nest." Short story.
              Signed Willa Cather. HM 6:12-13, 22-
              23. [Conclusion; check HM 6 (September
              1896) for complete entry.]

[1896]   "Nordica Has Returned." Editorial. Unsign-
               ed. HM 6:14.

               "Prodigal Salaries to Singers." Editorial.
               Unsigned. HM 6:14.
               W&P, pp. 315-16.

               "'Thine Eyes So Blue and Tender.'" Poem.
               Signed "Emily Vantell." HM 6:15.
               AT3. Rev. ed., p. 66.

               "Jingle: / Bobby Shafto." Poem. Signed
               "John Esten." HM 6:18.
               AT3. Rev. ed., p. 67.

        13 Review of Sol Smith Russell in A Bachelor's
               Romance. Unsigned. PL, p. 10.

Nov.   "The Origin of Thanksgiving." Article.
               Signed "Helen Delay." HM 6:8.

               "Death of George DuMaurier." Article. Un-
               signed. HM 6:11.
               W&P, pp. 316-18.

               "The Return of the Romantic Drama." Edito-
               rial. Unsigned. HM 6:12.
               W&P, p. 318.

               "My Horseman." Poem. Unsigned. HM 6:15.
               AT3. Rev. ed., p. 68.

        10 Review of Joseph Jefferson in Rip Van
               Winkle. Unsigned. PL, p. 6.
               W&P, pp. 422-23.

        24 Review of the Hollands in A Superfluous
               Husband and Colonel Carter of Carters-
               ville. Signed Willa. PL, p. 5.

        26 "Wee Winkie's Wanderings." Short story.

37

[1896]   Unsigned. <u>National Stockman</u> and <u>Farmer</u>,
             p. 18.
             <u>Vogue</u> 161 (June 1973):113.
             <u>Willa Cather Pioneer Memorial</u> and <u>Educa-
                tional Foundation Newsletter</u> 17 (Liter-
                ary issue, summer 1973):2-3.

Dec.   "The Three Holy Kings." Poem, a translation
             from Heine. Unsigned. <u>HM</u> 6:cover, 1.
             [Cover hand-lettered with illustration.]

             "The Burglar's Christmas." Short story.
             Signed "Elizabeth L. Seymour." <u>HM</u> 6:8-10.
             <u>CSF</u>, pp. 557-66.

             "'Ian Maclaren' as a Minister." Article.
             Unsigned. <u>HM</u> 6:12.

             "The Strategy of the Were-Wolf Dog." Short
             story. Signed Willa Cather. <u>HM</u> 6:13-14,
             24.
             <u>CSF</u>, pp. 441-48.

      1   Review of Hoyt's <u>A Milk White Flag</u>. Signed
             "Sibert." <u>PL</u>, p. 4.
             <u>W&P</u>, pp. 467-68.

      6   "The Passing Show." Massenet's <u>Eve</u>, E. M.
             Holland in <u>A Social Highwayman</u>, Cam-
             panini. Signed Willa Cather. <u>NSJ</u>, p. 13.
             <u>W&P</u>, pp. 377-79, 379-81.

      8   Review of <u>Thoroughbred</u>. Signed "Sibert."
             <u>PL</u>, p. 2.

     13   "The Passing Show." On Nordica and Jean de
             Reszke, Howells, <u>Princess Osra</u> drama-
             tized. Signed Willa Cather. <u>NSJ</u>, p. 13.
             <u>W&P</u>, pp. 381-84.

     15   Review of Frank Daniels in <u>Wizard of the</u>

[1896]   Nile by Victor Herbert. Signed "Sibert."
               PL, p. 6.
               W&P, pp. 385-86.

20 "The Passing Show." On Henry James's The
      Other House, Frank Daniels in Wizard of
      the Nile. Unsigned. NSJ, p. 13.
      W&P, pp. 551-53.

22 "Beautiful Anna Held." Article. Signed
      "Sibert." PL, p. 6.

24 "The Editor's Talk." Feature. Signed "The
      Editor." National Stockman and Farmer,
      p. 18.
      Willa Cather Pioneer Memorial and Educa-
      tional Foundation Newsletter 17 (Liter-
      ary issue, summer 1973):3-4. [Retitled
      "About Jim and Elsie."]

29 Review of James Herne's Shore Acres. Sign-
      ed "Sibert." PL, p. 6.
      W&P, pp. 469-71.

1897
Jan.   "Italo Campanini." Article. Unsigned. HM 6:
             11.

             "Books Old and New." On romances, Edna
             Lyall, children's classics. Signed "Helen
             Delay." HM 6:23.
             W&P, pp. 333-37.

3 "The Passing Show." On Anna Held. Signed
     Willa Cather. NSJ, p. 13.
     W&P, pp. 389-93.

5 Review of Jessie Bartlett Davis and The
     Bostonians in Robin Hood. Signed "Si-
     bert." PL, p. 4.

W&P, p. 386.

10 "The Passing Show." On Handel's Messiah,
     Anna Held and Henry C. Frick, Henry E.
     Abbey's career. Signed Willa Cather. NSJ,
     p. 13.
     W&P, pp. 471-73, 505-506.

12 Review of Otis Skinner in A Soldier of
     Fortune. Signed "Sibert." PL, p. 10.

17 "The Passing Show." On Jessie Bartlett
     Davis, Sunday music, Elia W. Peattie.
     Signed Willa Cather. NSJ, p. 13.
     W&P, pp. 506-507.

19 Review of Fanny Davenport in Gismonda.
     Signed "Sibert." PL, p. 10.

26 Review of My Friend from India. Signed
     "Sibert." PL, p. 8.
     W&P, pp. 468-69.

31 "The Passing Show." On Fanny Davenport in
     Sardou's Gismonda and La Tosca. Signed
     Willa Cather. NSJ, p. 13.
     W&P, pp. 424-26.

Feb.   "A Modern Man." Editorial on Prince Michael
        Hilkoff. Unsigned. HM 6:12.

        "Old Books and New." On romances, The Pris-
        oner of Zenda, Treasure Island. Signed
        "Helen Delay." HM 6:19.
        W&P, pp. 338-39.

 2 Review of Julia Marlowe in Romeo and
     Juliet. Unsigned. PL, p. 5.

 7 "The Passing Show." On Carreño in concert.
     Signed Willa Cather. NSJ, p. 13.

[1897]   <u>W&P</u>, pp. 397-400.

9 Review of <u>Pudd'nhead Wilson</u>. Signed
   "Sibert." <u>PL</u>, p. 4.
   <u>W&P</u>, pp. 477-78.

14 "The Passing Show." On Julia Marlowe as
   Juliet, E. S. Willard. Signed Willa
   Cather. <u>NSJ</u>, p. 13
   <u>W&P</u>, pp. 427-29.

23 Review of Margaret Mather in <u>Cymbeline</u>.
   Signed "Sibert." <u>PL</u>, p. 4.

28 "The Passing Show." On Nordica in concert,
   Sothern in <u>An Enemy to the King</u>. Signed
   Willa Cather. <u>NSJ</u>, p. 13.

Mar.   "The Carnegie Museum." Article. Signed
           Willa Cather. <u>HM</u> 6:1-4.

           "The Passing of 'The Duchess.'" Article.
           Unsigned. <u>HM</u> 6:7.

           "'Mark Twain's' Poverty." Editorial. Un-
           signed. <u>HM</u> 6:12.

           "The Sultan's Musical Taste." Editorial.
           Unsigned. <u>HM</u> 6:12.

           "Old Books and New." On <u>Kings in Exile</u>,
           <u>The Crime of Sylvestre Bonnard</u>, <u>Phroso</u>.
           Signed "Helen Delay." <u>HM</u> 6:16.
           <u>W&P</u>, pp. 340-43.

2 Review of <u>The Sporting Duchess</u>. Signed "Sibert." <u>PL</u>, p. 6.

4 Review of <u>Lohengrin</u>. Signed "A Woman Lover
   of Music." <u>PL</u>, p. 5.
   <u>W&P</u>, pp. 400-402.

41

[1897] 6   Review of Tannhäuser. Unsigned (in a pre-
fatory note author is described as "a
lady who wields a trenchant pen"). PL,
p. 6.
W&P, pp. 402-404.

7   "The Passing Show." On Margaret Mather in
Cymbeline, The Heart of Maryland. Signed
Willa Cather. NSJ, p. 13.
W&P, pp. 429-32.

9   Review of Nat Goodwin in An American Citi-
zen. Signed "Sibert." PL, p. 4.
Willa Cather Pioneer Memorial and Educational Foundation Newsletter 16 (Literary issue, summer 1972):1-2.

14   "The Passing Show." On Lohengrin and Tannhäuser. Signed Willa Cather. NSJ, p. 13.
W&P, pp. 404-408.

16   Review of Nethersole in Carmen. Signed
"Sibert." PL, p. 4.
Willa Cather Pioneer Memorial and Educational Foundation Newsletter 16 (Literary issue, summer 1972):2.

23   Review of DeWolf Hopper in El Capitan by
John Philip Sousa. Signed "Sibert." PL,
p. 4.
W&P, p. 387.

28   "The Passing Show." On Nethersole in Car-
men, Camille, and The Wife of Scarli.
Signed Willa Cather. NSJ, p. 13.
W&P, pp. 432-36.

Apr.   "A Resurrection." Short story. Signed Willa
Cather. HM 6:4-8.
Early Stories. Selected by Mildred R.
Bennett. New York: Dodd, Mead & Co.,

[1897]   1957, pp. 147-67.
              CSF, pp. 425-39.

              "The Byronic Renaissance." Editorial. Un-
                signed. HM 6:12.

              "German Opera in Pittsburgh." Editorial.
                Unsigned. HM 6:12.

              "Little Greece." Editorial. Unsigned. HM
                6:12.

              "Old Books and New." On Les Misérables, A
                Kentucky Cardinal. Signed "Helen Delay."
                HM 6:16.
                W&P, pp. 343-45.

         4   "The Passing Show." On Nat Goodwin in An
                American Citizen, DeWolf Hopper in El
                Capitan, Julia Marlowe. Signed Willa
                Cather. NSJ, p. 13.

         6   Review of Maude Adams and John Drew in
                Rosemary. Signed "Sibert." PL, p. 4.
                Willa Cather Pioneer Memorial and Educa-
                  tional Foundation Newsletter 16 (Liter-
                  ary issue, summer 1972):2-3.

        20   Review of Richard Mansfield in The Mer-
                chant of Venice. Signed "Sibert." PL,
                p. 9.
                Willa Cather Pioneer Memorial and Educa-
                  tional Foundation Newsletter 16 (Liter-
                  ary issue, summer 1972):3.

May   "Nursing as a Profession for Women." Arti-
                cle. Signed "Elizabeth L. Seymour." HM
                6:3-5.
                W&P, pp. 319-24.

              "King George of Greece." Editorial. Un-

                            43

[1897] signed. HM 6:12.

"Old Books and New." On David Copperfield,
Mark Twain, Mrs. Humphry Ward and George
Eliot, the imaginative boy. Signed "Helen
Delay." HM 6:18.
W&P, pp. 346-49.

2 "The Passing Show." On Maude Adams and John
Drew in Rosemary, Mansfield in The Mer-
chant of Venice. Signed Willa Cather.
NSJ, p. 13.
W&P, pp. 437-38, 439-41.

16 "The Passing Show." On Yvette Guilbert,
Kipling as bard. Signed Willa Cather.
NSJ, p. 13.
W&P, pp. 555-56.

23 "The Passing Show." On Calvé in concert.
Signed Willa Cather. NSJ, p. 13.
W&P, pp. 409-411.

25 Review of Lizzie Hudson Collier in Rosedale. Signed "Sibert." PL, p. 9.

30 "The Passing Show." On Lizzie Hudson
Collier in Rosedale, Mrs. Fiske in Tess
of the D'Urbervilles. Signed Willa
Cather. NSJ, p. 13.
W&P, pp. 443, 443-47.

June "Victoria's Ancestors." Article. Signed
Willa Cather. HM 6:1-4.
W&P, pp. 325-32.

"The Paper Age." Editorial. Unsigned. HM
6:12.

"Emma Calvé." Article. Unsigned. HM 6:13-
14.

44

[1897]   "Old Books and New." On Moore and Byron; a "simple recipe for making a novel à la Ouida." Signed "Helen Delay." HM 6:14. W&P, pp. 350-53.

1   Review of The People's King. Signed "Sibert." PL, p. 4.

July   "The Great Woman Editor of Paris." Article on Mme. Juliette Adam, editor of Nouvelle Revue. Unsigned. HM 6:8.

"The Prodigies." Short story. Signed Willa Cather. HM 6:9-11.
Courier, 10, 17 July 1897, pp. 4-5, 8-9.
Early Stories. Selected by Mildred R. Bennett. New York: Dodd, Mead & Co., 1957, pp. 169-85.
CSF, pp. 411-23.

"Not to the Queen's Taste." Editorial on Victoria's dislike of Melba. Unsigned. HM 6:12.

"Old Books and New." On Emerson, Hall Caine's The Bondman. Signed "Helen Delay." HM 6:14.
W&P, pp. 353-54.

31   "Nanette: An Aside." Short story. Signed Willa Cather. Courier, pp. 11-12.
HM 6 (August 1897):5-6.
Early Stories. Selected by Mildred R. Bennett. New York: Dodd, Mead & Co., 1957, pp. 93-102.
CSF, pp. 405-410.

Sept.   ["The Seine Divides old Paris Still"]. Poem. Unsigned (identified as "Inscription on the fly leaf of an old romance"). HM 6:14. [Some stanzas used in "Then

45

[1897]   Back to Ancient France Again"; see
Courier, 22 April 1899.]
W&P, p. 355.

"Old Books and New." On Gilbert Parker's
The Seats of the Mighty, Dicken' A Tale
of Two Cities. Signed "Helen Delay." HM
6:14.
W&P, pp. 355-57.

28   Review of Never Again. Signed "Sibert."
PL, p. 4.

Oct.   "Old Books and New." On Housman, Frances
Hodgson Burnett's A Lady of Quality,
Thackeray, Alice in Wonderland. Signed
"Helen Delay." HM 6:14.
W&P, pp. 358-61.

5   Review of Divorce by Augustin Daly. Signed
"Sibert." PL, p. 4.

15   "Books and Magazines." Reviews of Tales
from McClure's: Tales of Humor, Edgar
Allan Poe: Characteristic Short Stories,
Old Ebenezer by Opie Read, Hugh Wynne,
Free Quaker by S. Weir Mitchell. Unsign-
ed. PL, p. 2.

19   Review of The Prisoner of Zenda. Signed
"Sibert." PL, p. 4.

22   "Books and Magazines." Reviews of Captains
Courageous by Rudyard Kipling, The Days
of Jeanne d'Arc by Mary Hartwell Cather-
wood. Unsigned. PL, p. 2.

23   "The Passing Show." On the horse show,
Charles Stanley Reinhart. Signed Willa
Cather. Courier, pp. 8-9.
W&P, pp. 508-510, 510-12.

26   Review of The Wedding Day. Signed "Sibert."
     PL, p. 4.

30   "The Passing Show." On Sousa and Kipling,
     the Carnegie Prize committee, Will H. Low
     on Stevenson and Bouguereau. Signed Willa
     Cather. Courier, p. 3.
     W&P, pp. 387-89, 513-14, 562.

     "Anthony Hope's Lecture." Review. Signed
     "Sibert." PL, p. 6.

Nov.   "Old Books and New." On George Eliot's Mill
     on the Floss. Signed "Helen Delay." HM
     6:14.
     W&P, pp. 361-65.

5   "Books and Magazines." Reviews of For the
     Cause by Stanley Weyman and "How the
     Greeks Were Defeated" by Frederick Palm-
     er, Forum (November 1897). Unsigned. PL,
     p. 12.

6   "The Errand." Poem, a translation from
     Heine, in "The Passing Show." Signed
     Willa Cather. Courier, p. 2.
     W&P, p. 515.

     "The Passing Show." On Heine and Hugo,
     Evangelina Cisneros, Lillian Russell in
     The Wedding Day. Signed Willa Cather.
     Courier, p. 2.
     W&P, pp. 393-95, 515-17.

13 "The Passing Show." On Writers' Club dinner
     for Anthony Hope Hawkins and interview.
     Signed Willa Cather. Courier, pp. 2-3.
     W&P, pp. 564-70.

16 Review of Mrs. Fiske in Tess of the

[1897]   D'Urbervilles. Signed "Sibert." <u>PL</u>,
                p. 11.
                <u>W&P</u>, pp. 447-48.

       19   "Books and Magazines." Reviews of <u>The Charm</u>
            <u>and Other Drawing Room Farces</u> by Sir
            Walter Besant and Walter Pollock and <u>The</u>
            <u>Love Affairs of Some Famous Men</u>. Unsign-
            ed. <u>PL</u>, p. 4.

       20   "The Passing Show." On President McKinley
            in Pittsburgh, Campanari concert. Signed
            Willa Cather. <u>Courier</u>, pp. 2-3.
            <u>W&P</u>, pp. 517-21.

       23   Review of Belasco's <u>The Wife</u>. Signed "Si-
            bert." <u>PL</u>, p. 8.
            <u>W&P</u>, pp. 479-80.

       26   "Books and Magazines." Reviews of <u>The Lati-</u>
            <u>mers</u> by Henry McCook, <u>A Fountain Sealed</u>
            by Walter Besant, <u>Blown Away</u> by Richard
            Mansfield, <u>Thro' Lattice Windows</u> by Dr.
            W. J. Davidson. Unsigned. <u>PL</u>, p. 4.
            <u>Willa Cather Pioneer Memorial</u> and <u>Educa-</u>
                <u>tional Foundation Newsletter</u> 16 (Liter-
                ary issue, spring 1972):1-2.

       30   Review of <u>The Sporting Duchess</u>. Signed
            "Sibert." <u>PL</u>, p. 10.

Dec.   "Old Books and New." On William Allen
            White, Kipling's <u>Captains Courageous</u>.
            Signed "Helen Delay." <u>HM</u> 6:12.
            <u>W&P</u>, pp. 365-67.

            "<u>The Wandering Jew</u>." Review of Eugène Sue's
            novel. Signed "Helen Delay." <u>HM</u> 6:19.
            <u>W&P</u>, pp. 367-68.

       1   "With Nansen to the Pole." Article. Sign-

[1897]   ed "Sibert." <u>PL</u>, p. 2.

  4   "The Passing Show." On Victor Herbert's
      <u>Serenade</u>, Anton Seidl and the United
      Singers. Signed Willa Cather. <u>Courier</u>,
      p. 2.
      <u>W&P</u>, pp. 412, 525-26.

  11 ["Had You But Smothered That Devouring
      Flame"]. Poem, a translation of three
      stanzas from Alfred de Musset's "Mali-
      bran" in "The Passing Show." Signed
      Willa Cather. <u>Courier</u>, p. 2.
      <u>W&P</u>, pp. 451-52.

      "The Passing Show." On Minnie Maddern Fiske
      in <u>Tess of the D'Urbervilles</u>. Signed
      Willa Cather. <u>Courier</u>, pp. 2-3.
      <u>W&P</u>, pp. 448-52.

  14 Review of "Salt of the Earth." Signed
      "Sibert." <u>PL</u>, p. 4.

  18 "The Passing Show." On Writers' Club dinner
      for Fridtjof Nansen and interview. Sign-
      ed Willa Cather. <u>Courier</u>, pp. 4-5.
      <u>W&P</u>, pp. 521-25.

  25 "The Passing Show." On Nansen's views on
      literature, <u>New World</u> symphony, musi-
      cians' stories. Signed Willa Cather.
      <u>Courier</u>, pp. 2-3.
      <u>Prairie Schooner</u> 38 (winter 1964 / 65):
      344-45.
      <u>W&P</u>, pp. 413-14.

  26 "Phases of Alphonse Daudet." Article. Sign-
      ed "Sibert." <u>PL</u>, p. 16.

  28 Review of <u>The Lost Paradise</u>. Signed "Si-
      bert." <u>PL</u>, p. 4.

Jan.

"Old Books and New." On S. Weir Mitchell's
Hugh Wynne: Free Quaker, Anthony Hope's
Rupert of Hentzau, Charlotte Brontë's
Jane Eyre. Signed. "Helen Delay." _HM_
6:12.
_W&P_, pp. 369-72.

1   "The Passing Show." On Olive May in _White
Heather_, William Gillette's _Secret Ser-
vice_. Signed Willa Cather. _Courier_,
pp. 2-3.
_W&P_, pp. 480-81.

4   Review of Melba in _The Barber of Seville_.
Signed "Sibert." _PL_, p. 4.

7   "Books and Magazines." Reviews of _The
School for Saints_ by John Oliver Hobbes
(Pearl Craigie), _The Habitant_ by Wil-
liam H. Drummond. Unsigned. _PL_, p. 13.
_W&P_, pp. 570-71.

11 Review of William H. Crane in _A Virginia
Courtship_. Signed "Sibert." _PL_, p. 6.

18 Review of E. S. Willard in _Garrick_ by
Augustin Daly. Signed "Sibert." _PL_, p. 4.

22 "The Passing Show." On the death of Daudet.
Signed Willa Cather. _Courier_, pp. 2-3.
_W&P_, pp. 572-76.

28 "Books and Magazines." Reviews of _Reminis-
cences of William Wetmore Story_ by Mary
E. Phillips, _There is No Devil_ by Marius
Jokal (Maurus Jokai). Unsigned. _PL_, p. 5.
_W&P_, pp. 577-79.

29 "The Passing Show." On Melba in _The Barber
of Seville_, Yone Noguchi. Signed Willa

[1898]   Cather. _Courier_, p. 2.
            _W&P_, pp. 414-17, 579-80.

Feb.   "Old Books and New." On the death of ·
            Daudet, _Quo Vadis_?. Signed "Helen Delay."
            _HM_ 6:12.
            _W&P_, pp. 372-74.

      5   "The Passing Show." On Ethelbert Nevin's
            Carnegie Hall recital. Unsigned. _Courier_,
            pp. 3-4.
            _W&P_, pp. 533-38.

      6   "Miss Mould Talks." Interview. Unsigned.
            _PL_, p. 5.

      9   Review of _Ash Wednesday_, a farce. Unsigned.
            New York _Sun_, p. 7. [Probable; check _W&P_,
            p. 421.]

     11   Reviews of Modjeska in _Mary Stuart_ and of
            Way Down East. Unsigned. New York _Sun_,
            p. 7. [Probable; check _W&P_, 421.]
            _W&P_, pp. 457-59.

     19   "The Passing Show." On interviewing Ade-
            laide Mould [misspelled "Moned"], daugh-
            ter of Marion Manola. Unsigned. _Courier_,
            pp. 2-3.
            _W&P_, pp. 527-32.

     26   "The Passing Show." On E. S. Willard. Sign-
            ed Willa Cather. _Courier_, pp. 2-3.
            _W&P_, pp. 485-88.

Mar. 1   Review of Vesta Tilley in vaudeville.
            Signed "Sibert." _PL_, p. 10.

      4   "Books and Magazines." Reviews of _Going to
            War in Greece_ by Frederick Palmer and
            "English as Against French Literature" by

[1898]   Henry D. Sedgwick, _Atlantic_ (March 1898).
Signed "Sibert." _PL_, p. 8.
_W&P_, pp. 582-84.

5   "The Passing Show." On New York productions
of _The Lady of Lyons_, Ada Rehan in _The
Country Girl_, Modjeska in _Mary Stuart_.
Signed Willa Cather. _Courier_, pp. 2-3.
_W&P_, pp. 452-55, 455-57, 459-60.

11   "Books and Magazines." Reviews of _The Tales
of John Oliver Hobbes_ (Pearl Craigie),
The Story of Evangelina Cisneros by
Evangelina Cisneros and Karl Decker.
Signed "Sibert." _PL_, p. 4.
_W&P_, pp. 585-86.

12   "The Passing Show." On New York productions
of _The Tree of Knowledge_, _The Conquerors_.
Signed Willa Cather. _Courier_, pp. 2-3.
_W&P_, pp. 482-85.

18   "Books and Magazines." Review of _The Barn-
Stormers_ by Mrs. Harcourt Williamson.
Signed "Sibert." _PL_, p. 3.

19   "The Passing Show." On Melba, Nat Goodwin,
Vesta Tilley. Signed Willa Cather.
Courier, pp. 2-3.
_W&P_, pp. 395-97, 417-19.

25   "Books and Magazines." Reviews of _Across
the Salt Sea_ by John Bloundell-Burton,
_In the Midst of Life: Tales of Soldiers
and Civilians_ by Ambrose Bierce. Signed
"Sibert." _PL_, p. 9.
_W&P_, pp. 586-87.

29   Review of Mansfield in _The Devil's Disci-
ple_. Signed "Sibert." _PL_, p. 4.
_W&P_, pp. 489-90.

[1898]

Apr.   ["O! The World Was Full of the Summer
          Time"]. Poem, with a story "The Way
          of the World." Signed Willa Cather.
          HM 6:10.
          Courier, 19 August 1899, p. 8.
          CSF, p. 395.

          "The Way of the World." Short story.
          Signed Willa Cather. HM 6:10-11.
          Courier, 19 August 1899, pp. 9-10.
          CSF, pp. 395-404.

      8   "Books and Magazines." Reviews of The Ro-
          mance of Zion Chapel by Richard Le Gal-
          lienne, Woman's Bible, Volume II, by
          Elizabeth Cady Stanton. Signed "Sibert."
          PL, p. 11.
          W&P, pp. 538-41, 587-89.

      9   "The Passing Show." Letter to Nat Goodwin.
          Signed Willa Cather. Courier, p. 3.
          W&P, pp. 461-64.

     15   "Books and Magazines." Review of Fantasia
          by George Egerton. Signed "Sibert."
          PL, p. 14.

     16   "The Passing Show." On Mrs. Harcourt Wil-
          liamson's The Barn-Stormers. Signed
          Cather. Courier, p. 3.

     19   Review of Charles Coghlan in The Royal Box.
          Signed "Sibert." PL, p. 10.

     23   "The Passing Show." On Lieutenant Jenkins
          and the sinking of the Maine, Mansfield
          in The Devil's Disciple. Signed Willa
          Cather. Courier, pp. 3-4.
          W&P, pp. 544-46.

30 "The Passing Show." On Charles Coghlan's
The Royal Box. Signed Willa Cather.
Courier, pp. 3-4.
W&P, pp. 481-82.

May 6 "Books and Magazines." Reviews of A Bride
of Japan by Carlton Dawe, Here and There
and Everywhere by Mrs. E. W. Sherwood.
Signed "Sibert." PL, p. 9.
W&P, pp. 541-43.

27 "Books and Magazines." Review of The French
Market Girl by Emile Zola. Signed "Si-
bert." PL, p. 5.
W&P, pp. 592-94.

June 24 "Books and Magazines." Review of The Brown-
Laurel Marriage by Landis Ayr. Signed
"Sibert." PL, p. 5.

July 22 "Books and Magazines." Review of The Aure-
lian Wall and Other Poems by Bliss Carman. Signed "Sibert." PL, p. 6.
W&P, pp. 580-81.

Oct. 25 Review of The Bride Elect by John Philip
Sousa. Signed "Sibert." PL, p. 2.
W&P, pp. 610-11.

Nov. 1 Review of The Tree of Knowledge. Signed
"Sibert." PL, p. 11.

4 "Books and Magazines." Review of The Romance of the House of Savoy by Althea
Wiel. Signed "Sibert." PL, p. 13.

15 Review of Modjeska in Mary Stuart. Signed
"Sibert." PL, p. 6.
W&P, pp. 460-61.

[1898]
19 "Books and Magazines." Review of A Yankee
   Boy's Success by Harry S. Morrison, The
   Changeling by Sir Walter Besant. Signed
   "Sibert." PL, p. 5.

29 Review of Nat Goodwin in Nathan Hale by
   Clyde Fitch. Signed "Sibert." PL, p. 5.

Dec. 2 "Books and Magazines." Reviews of In the
   Cage by Henry James, Plays, Pleasant and
   Unpleasant by G. Bernard Shaw. Signed
   "Sibert." PL, p. 13.
   W&P, pp. 553-54, 595-97.

10 "Books and Magazines." Reviews of Dream
   Days by Kenneth Grahame, The Money Cap-
   tain by William Howard Payne, Ashes of
   Empire by Robert W. Chambers. Signed
   "Sibert." PL, p. 9.
   Willa Cather Pioneer Memorial and Educa-
      tional Foundation Newsletter 17 (Liter-
   ary issue, winter 1973):3-4.

20 Review of E. A. Sothern in The King's
   Musketeers. Signed "Sibert." PL, p. 8.

24 "The Passing Show." On Mrs. Fiske in A Bit
   of Old Chelsea and Love Will Find a Way.
   Signed Willa Cather. Courier, p. 3.

1899
Jan. 7 "The Passing Show." On Israel Zangwill's
   lecture, "The Drama as a Fine Art."
   Signed Willa Cather. Courier, p. 11.
   W&P, pp. 491-94.

10 Review of Julia Marlowe in The Countess
   Valeska. Signed "Sibert." PL, p. 10.

[1899]

14   "The Passing Show." On interviewing Mrs.
      Fiske. Signed Willa Cather. <u>Courier</u>,
      p. 3.
      <u>W&P</u>, pp. 660-64.

20   "Books and Magazines." Reviews of <u>Omar the
      Tentmaker</u> by Nathan Haskell Doyle, <u>The
      Borderlands</u> of <u>Society</u> by Charles B.
      Davis. Signed "Sibert." <u>PL</u>, p. 13.

21   "The Passing Show." On Nat Goodwin in Clyde
      Fitch's <u>Nathan Hale</u>. Signed Willa Cather.
      <u>Courier</u>, p. 4.
      <u>W&P</u>, pp. 667-68.

24   Review of <u>Mr. Barnes of New York</u>. Signed
      "Sibert." <u>PL</u>, p. 10.

28   "The Passing Show." On Julia Marlowe in <u>As
      You Like It</u> and <u>The Countess</u> Valeska.
      Signed Willa Cather. <u>Courier</u>, pp. 2-3.
      <u>W&P</u>, pp. 669-73.

Feb. 4   "The Passing Show." On Johnstone Bennett,
      Rosenthal concert, Sothern in <u>The King's
      Musketeers</u>. Signed Willa Cather. <u>Courier</u>,
      p. 3.
      <u>W&P</u>, pp. 495-97, 543-44, 611-13.

12   "Genius in Mire." Article on Richard Realf.
      Signed "Sibert." <u>PL</u>, p. 20.

18   "Books and Magazines." Review of <u>The Day's
      Work</u> by Rudyard Kipling. Signed "Si-
      bert." <u>PL</u>, p. 5.

25   "The Passing Show." On Richard Realf. Sign-
      ed Willa Cather. <u>Courier</u>, pp. 3-4.
      <u>W&P</u>, pp. 598-603.

[1899]
Mar. 4 "The Passing Show." On Kipling's A Day's
Work. Signed Willa Cather. Courier,
pp. 2-3.
W&P, pp. 555-61.

10 "Books and Magazines." Reviews of The Two
Standards by William Barry, The Maine by
Captain Charles D. Sigbee. Signed "Si-
bert." PL, p. 12.
W&P, pp. 590-91.

18 "The Passing Show." On Lizzie Hudson Collier in Jane, Maude Adams in The Little
Minister. Signed Willa Cather. Courier,
p. 5.
W&P, pp. 547-48, 673-75.

21 Review of Mansfield in Rostand's Cyrano de
Bergerac. Signed "Sibert." PL, p. 4.

31 "Books and Magazines." Review of Frank
Norris's McTeague. Signed "Sibert." PL,
p. 7.

Apr. 8 "The Passing Show." On Richard Realf, Frank
Norris's McTeague. Signed Willa Cather.
Courier, pp. 2-3.
W&P, pp. 603-605, 605-608.

15 "The Passing Show." On Rostand's Cyrano de
Bergerac. Signed Willa Cather. Courier,
pp. 2-3.
W&P, pp. 497-502.

22 ["Then Back to Ancient France Again"].
Poem. Signed W. C. Courier, p. 2.
[Variant stanzas in poem, HM 6 (Sep-
tember 1897).]
AT3. Rev. ed., p. 69.

22 "The Passing Show." On Mansfield as Cyrano.
Signed Willa Cather. Courier, pp. 2-3.
W&P, pp. 675-77.

"Books and Magazines." Reviews of A Daughter of the Vine by Gertrude Atherton,
'Ickery Ann and Other Girls and Boys by
Elia W. Peattie. Signed "Sibert." PL,
p. 5.
W&P, pp. 694-96.
Willa Cather Pioneer Memorial and Educational Foundation Newsletter 17 (Literary issue, winter 1973):4.

May "Richard Realf, Poet and Soldier." Article.
Signed "Helen Delay." HM 6:10-11.

2 Review of Francis Wilson in The Little
Corporal. Signed "Sibert." PL, p. 2.

27 "Books and Magazines." Reviews of The Per-
fect Wagnerite: A Commentary on the Ring
of the Nibelungs by G. Bernard Shaw and
Holland as Seen by Americans by James H.
Gore. Signed "Sibert." PL, p. 5.
W&P, pp. 617-18.

June 3 "Books and Magazines." Reviews of The Pro-
fessor's Daughter by Anna Farquhar, The
Wind Among the Reeds by Willaim Butler
Yeats, War Is Kind by Stephen Crane.
Signed "Sibert." PL, p. 6.
W&P, pp. 700-702, 705-706.

10 "The Passing Show." On the Metropolitan
Opera Company in Pittsburgh--Lohengrin.
Signed Willa Cather. Courier, p. 3.
W&P, pp. 619-23.

"Books and Magazines." Reviews of The

[1899]   Market Place by Harold Frederic, Oliver
              Cromwell: A History by Samuel Harraden
              Church. Signed "Sibert." PL, p. 5.
              W&P, pp. 709-711.

        17   "The Passing Show." On the Metropolitan
              Opera Company in Pittsburgh--Die Wal-
              küre. Signed Willa Cather. Courier,
              pp. 2-3.
              W&P, pp. 623-26.

              "Books and Magazines." Reviews of No. 5
              John Street by Richard Whiteing, More by
              Max Beerbohm. Signed "Sibert." PL, p. 5.
              W&P, pp. 696-97, 712-14.

July   1   "The Passing Show." On the death of Au-
              gustin Daly. Signed Willa Cather.
              Courier, p. 3.
              W&P, pp. 473-76.

              "Books and Magazines." Review of The Ven-
              geance of the Female by Marion Wilcox.
              Signed "Sibert." PL, p. 5.

        8   "Books and Magazines." Reviews of The
              Awakening by Kate Chopin, What Women Can
              Earn, and Outsiders: An Outline by Robert
              W. Chambers. Signed "Sibert." PL, p. 6.
              W&P, pp. 697-99.

        15   "The Passing Show." On Ethelbert Nevin,
              titled "An Evening at Vineacre." Signed
              Willa Cather. Courier, pp. 4-5.
              Ladies' Home Journal, November 1900,
              p. 11. [Parts of the above column
              are used in this article, "The Man Who
              Wrote 'Narcissus.'"]
              W&P, pp. 626-34.

              "Books and Magazines." Reviews of George

59

[1899]   Borrow: _Life_ _and_ _Correspondence_ (2 vols.)
              by William Knapp, _A_ _Silent_ _Singer_ by
              Clara Morris. Signed "Sibert." _PL_, p. 5.
              _W&P_, pp. 699-700, 714-17.

     22 "The Passing Show." On Nethersole in _The_
         Second _Mrs._ _Tanqueray._ Signed Willa
         Cather. _Courier_, pp. 5, 9.
         _W&P_, pp. 677-78.

         "Books and Magazines." Review of _A_ _Lost_
         Lady _of_ _Old_ _Years_ by John Buchan. Sign-
         ed "Sibert." _PL_, p. 6.

     29 "The Passing Show." On John Buchan's _A_ _Lost_
         Lady _of_ _Old_ _Years_, Arnold Bennett's _A_ _Man_
         from _the_ _North._ Signed Willa Cather.
         Courier, pp. 3-4.
         _W&P_, pp. 718-20, 721-22.

Aug. 26 "The Passing Show." On Chopin's _The_ _Awaken-_
          ing, Hewlett's _The_ _Forest_ _Lovers._ Signed
          Willa Cather. _Courier_, pp. 3-4.
          _W&P_, pp. 720-21.

Sept. 2 "The Passing Show." On Richard Whiteing's
          No. 5 John Street. Signed Willa Cather.
          Courier, pp. 3-4.

      16 "The Passing Show." On Zola's _Germinal_, Eden
          Phillpotts' _Children_ _of_ _the_ _Mist._ Signed
          Willa Cather. _Courier_, pp. 3-4.
          _W&P_, pp. 722-24, 724-27.

      30 "The Westbound Train." Short story. Signed
          Willa Cather. _Courier_, pp. 3-5.
          CSF, pp. 381-93.

Oct. 21 "The Passing Show." On Isobel Strong's lec-
          ture on Stevenson. Signed Willa Cather.
          Courier, p. 3.

                        60

[1899]   <u>W&P</u>, pp. 562-64.

28 "Books and Magazines." Reviews of <u>Strong as
     Death</u> by Guy de Maupassant, <u>The Vizier of
     the Two-Horned Alexander</u> by Frank Stock-
     ton, <u>The Mormon Problem</u> by George Seibel.
     Signed "Sibert." <u>PL</u>, p. 9.

Nov. 4 "The Passing Show." On Elia W. Peattie,
     Maupassant's <u>Strong as Death</u>. Signed
     Willa Cather. <u>Courier</u>, pp. 3-4.
     <u>W&P</u>, pp. 728-30, 730-32.

     "Books and Magazines." Reviews of <u>Blix</u> by
     Frank Norris, <u>La Princesse lointaine</u> by
     Edmond Rostand, <u>Where Angels Fear to
     Tread</u> by Morgan Robertson. Signed "Si-
     bert." <u>PL</u>, p. 5.

  7 Review of <u>The Christian</u> by Hall Caine.
     Signed "Sibert." <u>PL</u>, p. 10.

 11 "Books and Magazines." Review of <u>Active
     Service</u> by Stephen Crane. Signed "Si-
     bert." <u>PL</u>, p. 9.
     <u>W&P</u>, pp. 703-705.

 18 "Books and Magazines." Review of <u>Germinal</u>
     by Emile Zola. Signed "Sibert." <u>PL</u>, p. 9.
     <u>W&P</u>, pp. 732-33.

 25 "The Passing Show." On Hall Caine's <u>The
     Christian</u>, dramatized. Signed Willa
     Cather. <u>Courier</u>, pp. 2-3.

     "Books and Magazines." Reviews of <u>Cashel
     Byron's Profession</u> by G. Bernard Shaw,
     <u>Don Cosme</u> by Troilus Hilgarde Tyndale,
     <u>The Rubáiyát of Omar Kháyyám</u> translated
     by Mrs. H. M. Cadell, <u>The Future of the
     American Negro</u> by Booker T. Washington.

61

[1899]   Signed "Sibert." PL, p. 6.
              W&P, pp. 733-34, 734-36.

Dec.   "Some Pittsburgh Composers." Article.
              Signed "Helen Delay." HM 6:6-7.

        2   "The Passing Show." Letter to Joseph
              Jefferson. Signed Willa Cather. Courier,
              pp. 3-4.
              W&P, pp. 680-87.

              "Books and Magazines." Review of The
              Helpers by Francis Lynde. Signed "Si-
              bert." PL, p. 6.

        9   "Books and Magazines." Review of The
              Gentleman from Indiana by Booth Tarking-
              ton. Signed "Sibert." PL, p. 9.

       16   "The Passing Show." Letter to Lillian
              Nordica. Signed Willa Cather. Courier,
              p. 3.
              W&P, pp. 642-46.

              "Books and Magazines." Review of The Love
              Affairs of a Bibliomaniac by Eugene
              Field. Signed "Sibert." PL, p. 3.
              W&P, pp. 736-37.

       23   "The Passing Show." On Pinero's Trelawney
              of the Wells, Olive May. Signed Willa
              Cather. Courier, p. 2.
              W&P, pp. 678-80.

       30   "The Passing Show." On Joseffy and Pach-
              mann, titled "Two Pianists." Signed
              Willa Cather. Courier, p. 2.
              W&P, pp. 613-16.

Jan. 6 ["In That Voice What Darker Magic"]. Poem,
a translation "after Heine." Signed Willa
Cather. <u>Courier</u>, p. 2.
<u>W&P</u>, p. 646.

"The Passing Show." On Clara Butt. Signed
Willa Cather. <u>Courier</u>, pp. 2-3.
<u>W&P</u>, pp. 646-50.

  7 "A Talk with Hambourg." Signed "Sibert."
<u>PL</u>, p. 8.

  9 Review of Nethersole in <u>Sapho</u>. Signed "Sibert." <u>PL</u>, p. 4.
<u>W&P</u>, pp. 688-89.

13 "The Passing Show." On Frank Norris's <u>Blix</u>.
Signed Willa Cather. <u>Courier</u>, pp. 2-3.
<u>W&P</u>, pp. 702-703.

20 "The Passing Show." On Booth Tarkington's
<u>The Gentleman from Indiana</u>, titled "A
Popular Western Novel." Signed Willa
Cather. <u>Courier</u>, pp. 2-3.
<u>W&P</u>, pp. 737-40.

27 "The Passing Show." On Mark Hambourg,
titled "The Pianist of Pure Reason."
Signed Willa Cather. <u>Courier</u>, p. 3.
<u>W&P</u>, pp. 650-55.

Feb. 17 "The Passing Show." On Henry Irving and
Ellen Terry in <u>The Merchant of Venice</u>.
Signed Willa Cather. <u>Courier</u>, pp. 2-3.
<u>W&P</u>, pp. 689-92.

Mar. 3 "The Passing Show." On Francis Lynde's <u>The
Helpers</u>, titled "A Great Denver Novel,"
and on Stephen Phillips' <u>Paolo and Fran-
cesca</u>, titled "England's New Dramatic

[1900]   Poet." Signed Willa Cather. <u>Courier</u>,
          pp. 2-3.

    10   "The Passing Show." On A. E. Housman, ti-
          tled "A Lyric Poet." Signed Willa
          Cather. <u>Courier</u>, pp. 2-3.
          <u>W&P</u>, pp. 706-709.

    13   Review of the Kendals in <u>The Elder Miss
          Blossom</u>. Signed "Sibert." <u>PL</u>, p. 10.

    17   "The Passing Show." On Jane Addams' lec-
          ture on Tolstoi. Signed Willa Cather.
          <u>Courier</u>, pp. 3-4.
          <u>W&P</u>, pp. 743-45.

          "In the Night." Poem. Signed Willa Sibert
          Cather. <u>Library</u>, p. 16.
          <u>Courier</u>, 7 April 1900, p. 3.

    24   "The Passing Show." On the Kendals in <u>The
          Elder Miss Blossom</u>, Mary Johnston's <u>To
          Have and to Hold</u>. Signed Willa Cather.
          <u>Courier</u>, p. 3.
          <u>W&P</u>, pp. 740-43.

          "Thou Art the Pearl." Poem. Signed "John
          Charles Asten." <u>Library</u>, p. 16.
          <u>AT</u>, p. 45.
          <u>ATOP</u>, p. 37.
          <u>Commonweal</u> 13 (25 February 1931):465.
          Library ed. 3:174-75.
          <u>AT3</u>, p. 44.

          "Some Personages of the Opera." Article.
          Signed Willa Sibert Cather. <u>Library</u>,
          pp. 18-20.
          <u>W&P</u>, pp. 755-60.

    29   "'Grandmither, Think Not I Forget.'" Poem.
          Signed Willa Sibert Cather. <u>PL</u>, p. 2.

[1900]   Critic 36 (April 1900):308.
                Courier, 28 April 1900, p. 2.
                Current Literature 28 (May 1900):161.
                AT, pp. 9-10.
                Chicago Tribune, 23 May 1903, p. 9.
                   [Review.]
                Poet Lore 14 (October 1903):114.
                   [Review.]
                McClure's 32 (April 1909):649.
                Current Literature 47 (July 1909):106.
                The Home Book of Verse. Edited by Burton
                   E. Stevenson. New York: Henry Holt and
                   Co., 1912, pp. 1015-16.
                The Little Book of Modern Verse. Edited by
                   Jessie B. Rittenhouse. Boston: Houghton
                   Mifflin Company, 1913, pp. 75-77.
                The Answering Voice: One Hundred Love
                   Lyrics by Women. Selected by Sara
                   Teasdale. Boston: Houghton Mifflin
                   Company, 1917, pp. 108-110.
                ATOP, pp. 13-14.
                Library ed. 3:145-47.
                AT3, pp. 5-6.

Apr.   "Eric Hermannson's Soul." Short story.
                Signed Willa Sibert Cather. Cosmopolitan
                28:633-44.
                Early Stories. Selected by Mildred R.
                   Bennett. New York: Dodd, Mead & Co.,
                   1957, pp. 187-215.
                CSF, pp. 359-79.

      7   "The Passing Show." On Frank Norris, titled
                "An Heir Apparent." Signed Willa Sibert
                Cather. Courier, p. 3.
                W&P, pp. 746-49.

                "Aftermath" (Version 1). Poem. Signed Willa
                   Sibert Cather. Library, p. 22. [Version 2
                   in AT; see 1903.]
                AT3, p. 58. Revised ed., p. 57.

                                 65

14   "Out of Their Pulpits." Article on Pittsburgh clergy. Signed "Helen Delay."
<u>Library</u>, pp. 7-8.

"In the Garden." Poem. Signed Willa Sibert Cather. <u>Library</u>, p. 20.

21   "The Passing Show." On Mrs. Fiske in <u>Becky
Sharp</u>. Signed Willa Sibert Cather.
<u>Courier</u>, p. 3.
<u>W&P</u>, pp. 664-66.

"A Philistine in the Gallery." Article.
Signed "Goliath." <u>Library</u>, pp. 8-9.
<u>W&P</u>, pp. 760-64.

28   "The Dance at Chevalier's." Short story.
Signed "Henry Nicklemann." <u>Library</u>,
pp. 12-13.
<u>Early Stories</u>. Selected by Mildred R.
  Bennett. New York: Dodd, Mead & Co.,
  1957, pp. 217-29.
<u>CSF</u>, pp. 547-55.

May   12   "The Passing Show." On <u>The Barber of Se-
ville</u>, <u>Cavalleria Rusticana</u>, <u>Don Gio-
vanni</u>. Signed Willa Sibert Cather.
<u>Courier</u>, p. 11.
<u>W&P</u>, pp. 655-58.

"The Sentimentality of William Tavener."
Short story. Signed Willa Sibert Cather.
<u>Library</u>, pp. 13-14.
<u>Early Stories</u>. Selected by Mildred R.
  Bennett. New York: Dodd, Mead & Co.,
  1957, pp. 231-37.
<u>CSF</u>, pp. 353-57.

26   "Fleur de Lis." Poem. Signed "Clara Wood
Shipman." <u>Library</u>, p. 13. [Doubtful.]

June　2　"One of Our Conquerors." Article. Signed
　　　　　　"Henry Nicklemann." Library, pp. 3-4.
　　　　　　W&P, pp. 765-69.

　　　　9　"Letters to a Playwright." Article. Sign-
　　　　　　ed Willa Sibert Cather. Library, p. 7.
　　　　　　W&P, pp. 769-71.

　　　16　"The Affair at Grover Station." Short
　　　　　　story. Signed Willa Sibert Cather.
　　　　　　Library, pp. 3-4. [Concluded in Library,
　　　　　　23 June 1900, pp. 14-15.]
　　　　　　Courier, 7 July 1900, pp. 3-5, 8-9.
　　　　　　Early Stories. Selected by Mildred R.
　　　　　　　Bennett. New York: Dodd, Mead & Co.,
　　　　　　　1957, pp. 239-56.
　　　　　　CSF, pp. 339-52.

　　　　　　"Pittsburgh Matinee Driving Club." Article
　　　　　　on horse racing. Signed "Henry Nickle-
　　　　　　mann." Library, pp. 12-13.

　　　23　"A Love Fray." Poem. Signed Clara Wood
　　　　　　Shipman." Library, p. 13. [Doubtful.]

　　　　　　"When I Knew Stephen Crane." Article.
　　　　　　Signed "Henry Nicklemann." Library,
　　　　　　pp. 17-18.
　　　　　　Courier, 14 July 1900, pp. 4-5.
　　　　　　Prairie Schooner 23 (1949):231-36.
　　　　　　CY, pp. 22-24. [Brief excerpts.]
　　　　　　W&P, pp. 772-78.

　　　30　"Broncho Bill's Valedictory." Poem. Sign-
　　　　　　ed Willa Sibert Cather. Library, p. 6.
　　　　　　Courier, 14 July 1900, p. 3.
　　　　　　AT3. Revised ed., pp. 70-72.

July　7　"The Hottest Day I Ever Spent." Article.
　　　　　　Signed "George Overing." Library,

[1900]   pp. 3-4. [See NSJ, 12 August 1894.]
           W&P, pp. 778-82.

    7 "The Children's Part in a Great Library."
       Article on Carnegie Library. Signed "Hen-
       ry Nicklemann." Library, pp. 16-17.

   14 "The Personal Side of William Jennings
       Bryan." Article. Signed "Henry Nickle-
       mann." Library, pp. 13-15.
       Prairie Schooner 23 (1949):331-37.
       CY, pp. 21-22. [Brief excerpts.]
       Roundup: A Nebraska Reader. Compiled and
         edited by Virginia Faulkner. Lincoln:
         University of Nebraska Press, 1957,
         pp. 221-26.
       W&P, pp. 782-89.

       "The Lonely Sleep." Poem. Signed Willa
       Sibert Cather. Library, p. 18.

   28 "A Singer's Romance." Short story. Signed
       Willa Sibert Cather. Library, pp. 15-16.
       Early Stories. Selected by Mildred R.
         Bennett. New York: Dodd, Mead & Co.,
         1957, pp. 257-63.
       CSF, pp. 333-38.

       "A Chinese View of the Chinese Situation."
       Interview. Signed "Henry Nicklemann."
       Library, pp. 16-17.

Aug.   4 "Are You Sleeping, Little Brother? / To J.
          E. C." Poem. Signed W. S. C. Library,
          p. 14.
          Courier, 11 August 1900, p. 9.
          Willa Cather Pioneer Memorial and Educa-
            tional Foundation Newsletter 11 (fall
            1967):1.
          AT3. Revised ed., pp. 73-74.

[1900] 4 "A Houseboat on Land." Article. Signed
"Henry Nicklemann." <u>Library</u>, pp. 17-18.
<u>W&P</u>, pp. 789-91.

11 "The Conversion of Sum Loo." Short story.
Signed Willa Sibert Cather. <u>Library</u>,
pp. 4-6.
<u>Early</u> <u>Stories</u>. Selected by Mildred R.
Bennett. New York: Dodd, Mead & Co.,
1957, pp. 265-75.
<u>CSF</u>, pp. 323-31.

Nov. "The Man Who Wrote 'Narcissus.'" Article on
Ethelbert Nevin. Signed Willa Sibert
Cather. <u>Ladies'</u> <u>Home</u> <u>Journal</u> 17:11.
[Revises some sections of "An Evening at
Vineacre"; see <u>Courier</u>, 15 July 1899.]
<u>W&P</u>, pp. 634-37.

Dec. "Asphodel." Poem. Signed Willa Sibert
Cather. <u>Critic</u> 37:565.
<u>NSJ</u>, 17 December 1900, p. 4.
<u>AT</u>, p. 12.
<u>The</u> <u>Humbler</u> <u>Poets</u> (<u>Second</u> <u>Series</u>): <u>A</u>
<u>Collection</u> <u>of</u> <u>Newspaper</u> <u>and</u> <u>Periodical</u>
<u>Verse</u>, <u>1885-1910</u>. Compiled by Wallace
and Frances Rice. Chicago: A. C.
McClurg and Co., 1911, p. 126.
<u>AT3</u>, p. 8.

9 "A Statesman and Scholar." Article on death
of Senator Cushman K. Davis, <u>Hedda</u> <u>Gab-</u>
<u>ler</u>. Signed Willa Sibert Cather. Date-
line "Washington." <u>NSJ</u>, p. 9.

16 "The Poet to His Public." Poem. Signed
Willa Sibert Cather. <u>NSJ</u>, p. 19. [Known
later as "The Encore."]
<u>AT</u>, p. 36.
<u>ATOP</u>, p. 42.
Library ed. 3:181.

[1900]   AT3, p. 34.

16   "In Washington." On the opening session of
     the Senate, Carreño's concert. Signed
     Willa Sibert Cather. Dateline "Washing-
     ton." NSJ, p. 19.
     W&P, pp. 794-97.

22   "Winter Sketches in the Capital." On the
     opening of the Senate, Carreño concert,
     death of Senator Davis. Signed Willa
     Sibert Cather. Dateline "Washington,
     D. C." IPL, p. 6.

29   "Winter Sketches in the Capital." On Hedda
     Gabler. Signed Willa Sibert Cather. Date-
     line "Washington, D. C." IPL, p. 14.
     W&P, pp. 798-801.

30   "Washington in Olden Days." On English
     playwright Haddon Chambers, early life
     in Washington, Olga Nethersole, Christ-
     mas in Washington. Signed Willa Sibert
     Cather. Dateline "Washington, D. C."
     NSJ, p. 13.
     W&P, pp. 801-802.

1901
Jan.   5   "Winter Sketches in the Capital." On the
           Chinese minister to the United States,
           Wu T'ing-fang. Signed Willa Sibert
           Cather. Dateline "Washington, D. C." IPL,
           p. 22.
           W&P, pp. 803-806.

       6   "Jefferson, Painter Actor." On an exhibition
           of paintings by Joseph Jefferson. Signed
           Willa Sibert Cather. Dateline "Washing-
           ton, D. C." NSJ, p. 14.

12   "Winter Sketches in the Capital." On Joseph
      Jefferson. Signed Willa Sibert Cather.
      Dateline "Washington, D. C." IPL, p. 10.
      W&P, pp. 807-810.

13   "In the Corcoran Gallery." On racial stud-
      ies by Hubert Vos, Daniel Frohman inter-
      view. Signed Willa Sibert Cather. Date-
      line "Washington, D. C." NSJ, p. 9.
      W&P, pp. 811-12.

19   "Winter Sketches in the Capital." On early
      days in Washington and Hubert Vos's
      racial studies. Signed Willa Sibert
      Cather. Dateline "Washington, D. C." IPL,
      pp. 10-11.

20   "Claims Against Turkey." On settling of
      missionary claims in Turkey, members of
      the diplomatic corps. Signed Willa Si-
      bert Cather. Dateline "Washington." NSJ,
      p. 9.

26   "Winter Sketches in the Capital." On the
      diplomatic corps. Signed Willa Sibert
      Cather. Dateline "Washington, D. C." IPL,
      pp. 10-11.

27   "Bernhardt in Washington." On Bernhardt and
      Maude Adams in L'Aiglon, Rostand. Signed
      Willa Sibert Cather. Dateline "Washing-
      ton, D. C." NSJ, p. 9.
      W&P, pp. 813-17.

Feb.   2   "Winter Sketches in the Capital." On Sarah
             Bernhardt and Maude Adams in the title-
             role of Rostand's L'Aiglon. Signed Willa
             Sibert Cather. Dateline "Washington,
             D. C." IPL, pp. 10-11.

[1901] 4 "Second View of Bernhardt." On La Tosca
and Camille. Signed Willa Sibert Cather.
Dateline "Washington, D. C." NSJ, p. 8.
W&P, pp. 817-21.

9 "Winter Sketches in the Capital." On
various aspects of Washington and the
White House. Signed Willa Sibert Cather.
Dateline "Washington, D. C." IPL,
pp. 8-9.

10 "Seton-Thompson at Tea." On Ernest Seton-
Thompson, Pittsburgh Symphony Orchestra,
death of Queen Victoria. Signed Willa
Sibert Cather. Dateline "Washington,
D. C." NSJ, p. 9.
W&P, pp. 822-24.

16 "Winter Sketches in the Capital." On Ernest
Seton-Thompson, Victor Herbert and the
Pittsburgh Symphony Orchestra. Signed
Willa Sibert Cather. Dateline "Washing-
ton, D. C." IPL, p. 8.

17 "The Charm of Washington." On the inhabi-
tants and sights, White House souvenirs.
Signed Willa Sibert Cather. Dateline
"Washington, D. C." NSJ, p. 9.

23 "The Gridiron Club Dinner." Article. Signed Willa Sibert Cather. Dateline "Washington, D. C." IPL, p. 12.

24 "Washington Gridiron Club." On annual Grid-
iron dinner, musical debut of Marquis
Francesco de Sousa and Clara Clemens.
Signed Willa Sibert Cather. Dateline
"Washington, D. C." NSJ, p. 9.

Mar. 3 "In Washington." On the poetry of Helen
Hay, the career of Mrs. E. D. E. N.

72

[1901]   Southworth. Signed Willa Sibert Cather.
              Dateline "Washington, D. C." NSJ, p. 12.

    9 "The Gay Lord Quex." Review of Pinero's
       play. Signed Willa Sibert Cather. Date-
       line "Washington, D. C." IPL, pp. 8-9.
       W&P, pp. 825-28.

    10 "In Washington." Review of Pinero's The Gay
        Lord Quex. Signed Willa Sibert Cather.
        Dateline "Washington, D. C." NSJ, p. 13.

    16 "Literature in the Capital." On Helen Hay's
        poetry, Edna [Emma] Southworth. Signed
        Willa Sibert Cather. Dateline "Washing-
        ton, D. C." IPL, pp. 8-9.
        W&P, pp. 828-32.

    17 "Hunting the North Pole." On the Baldwin-
        Ziegler expedition, Count Cassini's col-
        lections. Signed Willa Sibert Cather.
        Dateline "Washington, D. C." NSJ, p. 13.
        W&P, pp. 832-35.

    24 "Music." Ethelbert Nevin obituary. Sign-
        ed Willa Sibert Cather. NSJ, p. 13.
        W&P, pp. 637-42.

    30 "Jack-a-Boy." Short story. Signed Willa
        Sibert Cather. Saturday Evening Post 173:
        4-5, 25.
        Prairie Schooner 33 (1959):77-87.
        CSF, pp. 311-22.
        Friend of My Springtime: A Classic Story
        of Friendship. Illustrated by Arlene
        Noel with an introduction by Robert
        Aldace Wood. Kansas City, Missouri:
        Hallmark Cards, Inc., 1974. [No indi-
        cation of the original title given.]

May   "In Media Vita." Poem. Signed Willa Sibert Cather. <u>Lippincott's</u> 67:623.
<u>AT</u>, p. 21.
<u>ATOP</u>, p. 25.
<u>AT3</u>, p. 17.

June   "El Dorado: A Kansas Recessional." Short
story. Signed Willa Sibert Cather. <u>New
England Magazine</u>, new series, 24:357-69.
<u>CSF</u>, pp. 293-310.

July   20   "Comment and Commentary." On Western rail-
roads, Ernest Seton-Thompson. Signed
Willa Sibert Cather. <u>Courier</u>, p. 3.
<u>W&P</u>, pp. 837-39.

Aug.   10   "Observations." Editorial comment on: "Real
Strike Instigators" [on the incidence of
steel strikes], "Lax Denver Law" [poli-
tics and municipal corruption], "A
Dramatized Omar" [George Seibel's play
intended for Richard Mansfield], "Constant's Victoria" [unpopularity of Benjamin Constant's portrait of the queen],
"Edward MacDowell," "A New Drought Theo-
ry," "[William M.] Chase," "Chicago Art
Institute," "The Deterioration of a Com-
poser" [Victor Herbert]. Signed Willa Sibert Cather. <u>Courier</u>, pp. 1-3.
<u>W&P</u>, pp. 839-41, 841-42, 842-46, 855.

"Review of Eden Phillpotts' <u>Sons of the
Morning</u>. Signed Willa Sibert Cather.
<u>Courier</u>, p. 7.
<u>W&P</u>, pp. 846-48.

17   "Observations." Editorial comment on:
"Schley's Accuser" [Admiral W. S. Schley
accused of cowardice by Edgar S. McClay],
"A Tragedy of Environment" [on the Dow-

[1901]   ager Empress Frederick of Germany],
"Small Town Funerals," "Will White or
Funston?," "A New Library Line." Signed
Willa Sibert Cather. Courier, pp. 1-3.
W&P, pp. 849-50, 851-52, 853.

       24   "Observations." Editorial comment on: "With
David Nation" [supporting his suit for
divorce from Carry Nation], "Henry of
Orleans" [on the death of the Duc d'Or-
léans], "The Real Homestead," "Rodin's
Victor Hugo," "Train News Boys," "Forms
of Food Adulteration," "J. Pierpont Mor-
gan," "A Fore Runner" [Kipling], "Warm
Praise for [Charles] Dawes" [comptroller
of the currency retiring to run for the
Senate], "Duse and 'Il Fuoco.'" Signed
Willa Sibert Cather. Courier, pp. 1-3.
W&P, pp. 851, 853-54, 855-58, 858-59,
859-60, 860-62.

Sept.   "Winter at Delphi." Poem. Signed Willa Si-
bert Cather. Critic 39:269.
AT, p. 26.
New York Times Saturday Review, 20 June
1903, p. 434. [Review.]
ATOP, pp. 22-23.
Library ed. 3:157-58.
AT3, pp. 22-23.

Nov.   17   "The Philistine in the Art Gallery." Article. Signed "Henry Nicklemann." PG, p. 6.
W&P, pp. 864-67.

       24   "Popular Pictures." Article. Signed "Henry
Nicklemann." PG, p. 6.
W&P, pp. 867-69.

Dec.   8   "Pittsburgh's Mulberry Street." Article.
Signed "Henry Nicklemann." PG, Section V,
p. 5.

[1901]   W&P, pp. 870-74.

        22   "The Christmas Side." Article. Signed
             "Henry Nicklemann." PG, Section IV, p. 1.

1902
Jan.   4   "Arcadian Winter." Poem. Signed Willa Si-
            bert Cather. Harper's Weekly 46:24. [Un-
            signed, but Willa Sibert Cather is in the
            list of "Contributors to this number."]
            High School Journal [Pittsburgh Central
              High School] 7 (January 1902):1.
            Courier, 18 January 1902, p. 8.
            AT, pp. 15-16.
            ATOP, pp. 38-39.
            Library ed. 3:176-77.
            AT3, pp. 11-12.

Mar.   2   "Stage Celebrities Who Call Pittsburgh
            Home." Article. Signed "Henry Nickle-
            mann." PG, p. 8.

Apr.   "The Namesake / To W. L. B. of the Thirty-
            Fifth Virginia" [or "To W. S. B. of the
            Thirty-Third Virginia"]. Poem. Signed
            Willa Sibert Cather. Lippincott's 69:482.
            Courier, 12 April 1902, p. 3.
            AT, pp. 28-29. [With variant subtitle.]
            AT3, pp. 25-26.

       13   "A School for Servants." Article. Signed
            "Henry Nicklemann." PG, Section IV, p. 6.

June   "The Professor's Commencement." Short
            story. Signed Willa Sibert Cather. New
            England Magazine, new series, 26:481-88.
            CSF, pp. 283-91.

       15   "Pittsburgh's Richest Chinaman." Article.
            Signed "Henry Nicklemann." PG, magazine

[1902]   section, p. 5.

26   "The Night Express." Poem. Signed Willa S.
     Cather. Youth's Companion 76:328.
     NSJ, 20 July 1902, p. 12.
     PG, 3 August 1902, p. 12.
     AT, pp. 38-39.
     Youth's Companion. Edited by Lovell
       Thompson. Boston: Houghton Mifflin Co.,
       1954, pp. 275-76.
     AT3, pp. 36-37.

July   "In Rose Time." Poem. Signed Willa Sibert
     Cather. Lippincott's 70:97.
     PG, 13 July 1902, p. 2.
     AT, p. 11.
     Lincoln Star, 30 October 1921, p. 7.
     ATOP, pp. 31-32.
     Golden Book V (1927):723. [Last seven
       lines only.]
     Library ed. 3:167-68.
     AT3, p. 7.

13   "First Glimpse of England." Travel letter
     on arrival in Liverpool. Signed Willa S.
     Cather. NSJ, p. 4.
     WCE, pp. 5-11.
     W&P, pp. 890-93.

20   "A Visit to Old Chester." Travel letter.
     Signed Willa S. Cather. NSJ, p. 11.
     WCE, pp. 15-22.
     W&P, pp. 893-97.

27   "Out of the Beaten Track." Travel letter on
     Shropshire and A. E. Housman. Signed
     Willa S. Cather. NSJ, p. 11.
     WCE, pp. 27-34.
     W&P, pp. 897-901.

Aug.   3   "The Canal Folk of England." Travel letter.

77

[1902]   Signed Willa Sibert Cather. <u>NSJ</u>, p. 11.
              <u>WCE</u>, pp. 38-49.
              <u>W&P</u>, pp. 901-906.

    10   "Seeing Things in London." Travel letter.
         Signed Willa Sibert Cather. <u>NSJ</u>, p. 11.
         <u>WCE</u>, pp. 54-64.
         <u>W&P</u>, pp. 907-911.

         "The Hotel Child." Article. Signed Willa
         Sibert Cather. <u>PG</u>, magazine section,
         p. 4.
         <u>W&P</u>, pp. 874-79.

    17   "The Kensington Studio." Travel letter on
         Burne-Jones. Signed Willa S. Cather. <u>NSJ</u>,
         p. 11.
         <u>WCE</u>, pp. 70-79.
         <u>W&P</u>, pp. 912-17.

    24   "Merry Wives of Windsor." Travel letter on
         Beerbohm Tree's revival of The <u>Merry</u>
         <u>Wives</u> <u>of</u> <u>Windsor</u>. Signed Willa S. Cather.
         <u>NSJ</u>, p. 16.
         <u>WCE</u>, pp. 83-89.
         <u>W&P</u>, pp. 917-20.

         "Lives in a Streetcar All Year Round."
         Article. Signed "Henry Nicklemann." <u>PG</u>,
         Section IV, p. 2.

    31   "Dieppe and Rouen." Travel letter. Signed
         Willa S. Cather. <u>NSJ</u>, p. 16.
         <u>WCE</u>, pp. 93-100.
         <u>W&P</u>, pp. 920-24.

         "The Strangest Tribe of Darkest England."
         Article. Signed Willa Sibert Cather. <u>PG</u>,
         magazine section, p. 4.

Sept. 14   "Two Cemeteries in Paris." Travel letter

[1902]   on Montmartre and Père-Lachaise. Signed
                Willa S. Cather. NSJ, p. 18.
                WCE, pp. 105-114.
                W&P, pp. 924-29.

       21   "One Sunday at Barbizon." Travel letter.
                Signed Willa S. Cather. NSJ, p. 18.
                WCE, pp. 119-27.
                W&P, pp. 929-33.

       28   "The Old City of the Popes." Travel letter
                on Avignon. Signed Willa S. Cather. NSJ,
                p. 15.
                WCE, pp. 132-41.
                W&P, pp. 934-39.

Oct.   "The Treasure of Far Island." Short story.
                Signed Willa Sibert Cather. New England
                Magazine, new series, 27:234-49.
                Prairie Schooner 38 (winter 1964/1965):
                  323-43.
                CSF, pp. 265-82.

        5   "Country of the Fabulous." Travel letter on
                Marseilles and Hyères. Signed Willa S.
                Cather. NSJ, p. 15.
                WCE, pp. 144-51.
                W&P, pp. 939-42.

       12   "In a Principality of Pines." Travel letter
                on Le Lavandou. Signed Willa S. Cather.
                NSJ, p. 15.
                WCE, pp. 154-62.
                W&P, pp. 942-46.

       19   "In the Country of Daudet." Travel letter on
                Monte Carlo, the Provençal countryside,
                Arles. Signed Willa S. Cather. NSJ, p. 9.
                WCE, pp. 168-78.
                W&P, pp. 946-52.

[1902]

Nov. 30 "Pittsburgh Authors Known to Fame." Arti-
           cle. Signed "Henry Nicklemann." <u>PG</u>,
           literary section, pp. 20-21.

       "Poets of Our Younger Generation." Article.
       Signed Willa Sibert Cather. <u>PG</u>, literary
       section, p. 24.
       <u>W&P</u>, pp. 879-88.

1903

Jan.   "'A Death in the Desert.'" Short story.
           Signed Willa Sibert Cather. <u>Scribner's</u>
           33:109-121. [No quotation marks around
           the title in this version.]
           <u>TG</u>, pp. 111-54. [Revised from <u>Scribner's</u>
             version.]
           <u>YBM</u>, pp. 273-303. [Revised further.]
           <u>TG</u>. Signet Classics ed., pp. 65-86.
             [Original <u>TG</u> version with spelling
             and punctuation silently altered.]
           <u>CSF</u>, pp. 199-217.[Original <u>TG</u> version.]

Apr.   <u>April Twilights</u>. Poetry Collection. Boston:
           R. G. Badger.
           <u>ATOP</u>. [Reprints some poems from this
             collection; check individual poem
             titles.]
           Library ed. 3:141-216. [Reprints some
             poems; check individual poem titles.]
           <u>AT3</u>. [Reprints the whole collection.]

       "Dedicatory." Poem. <u>AT</u>, p. [3].
           <u>Prairie Schooner</u> 38 (winter 1964.1965):
             322.
           <u>AT3</u>, p. 3.

       "Mills of Montmartre." Poem. <u>AT</u>, pp. 13-14.
           <u>Poet Lore</u> 14 (winter 1903):114-115.
             [Review.]

[1903]   AT3, pp. 9-10.

"The Hawthorn Tree." Poem. AT, p. 17.
   Poet Lore 14 (winter 1903):115. [Re-
      view.]
   The Answering Voice: Love Lyrics by
      Women. Selected by Sara Teasdale.
      Boston: Houghton Mifflin Company,
      1917, p. 34.
   ATOP, p. 17.
   Published as a song with music by
      Jessie L. Pease, New York, 1923.
   Rapin, René. Willa Cather. New York:
      Robert M. McBride & Co., 1930, p. 15.
   Library ed. 3:152.
   AT3, p. 13.

"Sleep, Minstrel, Sleep." Poem. AT, p. 18.
   ATOP, p. 30.
   Library ed. 3:165-66.
   AT3, p. 14.

"Fides, Spes." Poem. AT, p. 19.
   McClure's 32 (February 1909):362.
   ATOP, p. 15.
   Library ed. 3:148-49.
   AT3, p. 15.

"The Tavern." Poem. AT, p. 20.
   New York Times Saturday Review, 20 June
      1903, p. 434. [Review.]
   McClure's 31 (August 1908):419.
   ATOP, p. 16.
   Library ed. 3:150-51.
   AT3, p. 16.

"Antinous." Poem. AT, p. 22.
   ATOP, p. 20.
   Library ed. 3:155.
   AT3, p. 18.

[1903]   "Paradox." Poem. <u>AT</u>, p. 23.
    <u>ATOP</u>, p. 24.
    Library ed. 3:159.
    <u>AT3</u>, p. 19.

"Provençal Legend." Poem. <u>AT</u>, pp. 24-25.
    <u>McClure's</u> 33 (September 1909):519.
    <u>ATOP</u>, pp. 40-41.
    Library ed. 3:178-80.
    <u>AT3</u>, pp. 20-21.

"On Cydnus." Poem. <u>AT</u>, p. 27.
    <u>PG</u>, 26 April 1903, section 2, p. 4.
    [Review.]
    <u>Commonweal</u> 13 (25 February 1931):466.
    <u>AT3</u>, p. 24.

"Lament for Marsyas." Poem. <u>AT</u>, p. 30.
    <u>McClure's</u> 30 (February 1908):453.
    <u>ATOP</u>, p. 27. [Last stanza omitted.]
    Library ed. 3:161-62. [<u>ATOP</u> version.]
    <u>AT3</u>, pp. 27-28. [<u>AT</u> version.]

"White Birch in Wyoming." Poem. <u>AT</u>, p. 31.
    <u>AT3</u>, p. 29.

"I Sought the Wood in Winter." Poem. <u>AT</u>,
    pp. 32-33.
    <u>ATOP</u>, pp. 28-29.
    <u>Golden Book</u> 13 (January 1931):70. [Third
      stanza only.]
    Library ed. 3:163-64.
    Greenslet, Ferris. <u>Under the Bridge</u>.
      Boston: Houghton Mifflin Company, 1943,
      p. 116. [The last eight lines only.]
    <u>AT3</u>, pp. 30-31.

"Evening Song." Poem. <u>AT</u>, p. 34.
    <u>McClure's</u> 29 (August 1907):365.
    <u>ATOP</u>, p. 26.
    Library ed. 3:160.

[1903]   AT3, p. 32.

"Eurydice." Poem. AT, p. 35.
  Commonweal 13 (25 February 1931):465.
  AT3, p. 33.

"The Encore." [See original title, "The
  Poet to His Public," NSJ, 16 December
  1900.]

"London Roses." Poem. AT, p. 37.
  McClure's 34 (November 1909):61.
  ATOP, p. 21.
  Library ed. 3:156.
  AT3, p. 35.

"Prairie Dawn." Poem. AT, p. 40.
  Dial 35 (16 July 1903):40-41.
  McClure's 31 (June 1908):229.
  NSJ, 10 June 1917, p. 3-c.
  ATOP, p. 35.
  Rapin, René. Willa Cather. New York:
    Robert M. McBride & Co., 1930, p. 16.
  Commonweal 13 (25 February 1931):466.
  Library ed. 3:172.
  Daiches, David. Willa Cather. Ithaca:
    Cornell University Press, 1951, p. 177.
  AT3, p. 38.

"Aftermath" (Version 2). Poem. AT, p. 40.
  PG, 26 April 1903, sec. 2, p. 4. [Re-
    view.]
  ATOP, p. 36.
  Library ed. 3:173.
  AT3, p. 39.

"Thine Advocate." Poem. AT, p. 41.
  AT3, p. 40.

"Poppies on Ludlow Castle." Poem. AT,
  pp. 42-43.

83

[1903]   ATOP, pp. 33-34.
                Library ed. 3:169-71.
                AT3, pp. 41-42.

"Sonnet." Poem. AT, p. 44.
  Commonweal 13 (25 February 1931):464.
  AT3, p. 43.

"From the Valley." Poem. AT, p. 46.
  AT3, p. 45.

"I Have No House for Love to Shelter Him."
Poem. AT, p. 47.
  Poet Lore 16 (summer 1905):50.
  AT3, p. 46.

"The Poor Minstrel." Poem. AT, pp. 48-49.
  McClure's 36 (February 1911):376.
  ATOP, pp. 18-19.
  Library ed. 3:153-54.
  AT3, pp. 47-48.

"Paris." Poem. AT, p. 50.
  AT3, p. 49.

"Song." Poem. AT, p. 51.
  ATOP, p. 43.
  AT3, p. 50.

"L'Envoi." Poem. AT, p. 52.
  The Humbler Poets (Second Series): A
    Collection of Newspaper and Periodical
    Verse, 1885-1910. Compiled by Wallace
    and Frances Rice. Chicago: A. C.
    McClurg and Co., 1911, p. 248.
  The Home Book of Verse. Edited by Burton
    E. Stevenson. New York: Henry Holt and
    Co., 1912, pp. 3217-18.
  ATOP, p. 44.
  Commonweal 13 (25 February 1931):465.
  Library ed. 3:182.

[1903]   _AT3_, p. 51.

Nov. 29 "The 100 Worst Books and They That Read
          Them." Article. Signed Willa Sibert
          Cather. _PG_, literary section, pp. 11, 14.
          _W&P_, pp. 961-64. [The title is given here
          erroneously as "The 100 Worst Books and
          They That Wrote Them."]

1904
Feb.   "A Wagner Matinée." Short story. Signed
          Willa Sibert Cather. _Everybody's Maga-
          zine_ 10:325-28.
          _TG_, pp. 193-210. [Revised.]
          YBM, pp. 235-47. [Further revisions.]
          Book of Modern Short Stories. Edited by
            Dorothy Brewster. New York: Macmillan
            Co., [1929], pp. 228-35. [_YBM_ version.]
          Library ed. 6:247-61. [Further re-
            visions.]
          Scholastic 32 (30 April 1938):17E-19E.
            [Library ed. version.]
          _TG_. Signet Classics ed., pp. 107-115.
            [Original _TG_ version with spelling
            and punctuation silently altered.]
          CSF, pp. 235-42. [Original _TG_ version.]

1905
Jan.   "The Sculptor's Funeral." Short story.
          Signed Willa Sibert Cather. _McClure's_
          24:329-36.
          _TG_, pp. 55-84. [Minor revisions.]
          YBM, pp. 248-72. [Further revisions.]
          Book of Modern Short Stories. Edited by
            Dorothy Brewster. New York: Macmillan
            Co., [1929], pp. 76-90. [_YBM_ version.]
          Golden Book 19 (February 1934):162-72.
            [_YBM_ version.]
          Library ed. 6:263-89. [Minor revisions.]

[1905]   TG. Signet Classics ed., pp. 35-49.
                 [Original TG version with spelling
                 and punctuation silently altered.]
                CSF, pp. 173-85. [Original TG version.]

Mar.   The Troll Garden. Short story collection.
                New York: McClure, Phillips & Co.

                New American Library reprint. New York:
                Signet Classics, 1961. [Not listed as
                a new edition and no note on editing,
                but with approximately seven hundred
                silent alterations.]

                "Flavia and Her Artists." Short story. TG,
                  pp. 1-54.
                  TG. Signet Classics ed., pp. 7-34. [Punc-
                    tuation and spelling silently altered.]
                  CSF, pp. 149-72.

                "The Garden Lodge." Short story. TG,
                  pp. 85-110.
                  TG. Signet Classics ed., pp. 51-63.
                   [Silent alterations.]
                  CSF, pp. 187-97.

                "The Marriage of Phaedra." Short story. TG,
                  pp. 155-92.
                  TG. Signet Classics ed., pp. 87-105.
                   [Silent alterations.]
                  CSF, pp. 219-34.

                "Paul's Case." Short story. (Originally
                  subtitled "A Study in Temperament.") TG,
                  pp. 211-53.
                  McClure's 25 (May 1905):74-83. [Changes
                    and cuts; see CSF bibliography for
                    discussion.]
                  YBM, pp. 199-234. [TG version revised.]
                  Contemporary Short Stories. Edited by
                    Kenneth A. Robinson. Boston: Houghton

                              86

[1905] Mifflin Co., [1924], pp. 44-69. [YBM version.]

Golden Book 5 (May 1927):681-90. [YBM version.]

Library ed. 6:207-245. [Revisions on YBM version.]

Five Stories. New York: Vintage Books, 1956, pp. 149-74. [YBM version.]

TG. Signet Classics ed., pp. 117-38. [Silent alterations.]

The Britannica Library of Great American Writing. 2 vols. Edited by Louis Untermeyer. Chicago: Britannica Press, 1960, pp. 1147-64. [YBM version.]

CSF, pp. 243-61. [YBM version.]

1907 Milmine, Georgine. The Life of Mary Baker G. Eddy, and the History of Christian Science. McClure's 28 (January, February, March, April 1907):227-42, 339-54, 506-524, 608-627; McClure's 29 (May, July, August, September, October 1907):97-116, 333-48, 447-62, 567-81, 688-99; McClure's 30 (February, March, April 1908):387-401, 577-90, 699-712; McClure's 31 (May, June 1908):16-31, 179-89. [Check entry for book publication in 1909; Stewart Hudson's introduction to the 1971 edition describes Cather's participation in the editing and writing.]

Reprinted as book. New York: Doubleday, Page & Co., 1909.

Mar. "The Namesake." Short story. McClure's 28: 492-97.

CSF, pp. 137-46.

June "The Profile." Short story. McClure's 29: 135-40.

CSF, pp. 125-35.

[1907]

Aug.   "The Willing Muse." Short story. <u>Century</u>
           74:550-57.
           <u>CSF</u>, pp. 113-23.

Oct.   "Eleanor's House." Short story. <u>McClure's</u>
           29:623-30.
           <u>CSF</u>, pp. 95-111.

Nov.   "Autumn Melody." Poem. <u>McClure's</u> 30:106.
           <u>ATOP</u>, p. 55.
           Library ed. 3:197.

Dec.   "The Star Dial." Poem. <u>McClure's</u> 30:202.
           [Subtitled "A Variation upon a Theme of
           Sappho's"; see Colby Library collection.]

1908

Dec.   "On the Gulls' Road." Short story. <u>Mc-</u>
           <u>Clure's</u> 32:145-52. [Originally sub-
           titled "The Ambassador's Story."]
           <u>CSF</u>, pp. 79-94.

1909   Milmine, Georgine. <u>The Life of Mary Baker</u>
           <u>G. Eddy, and the History of Christian</u>
           <u>Science.</u> New York: Doubleday, Page & Co.
           [See edition below for Stewart Hudson's
           introduction describing Cather's part
           in the editing and writing.]

           Edition with Cather listed as editor,
           introduction by Stewart Hudson. Grand
           Rapids, Michigan: Baker Book House, 1971.

Apr.   "The Enchanted Bluff." Short story.
           <u>Harper's</u> 118:774-81.
           <u>Five Stories.</u> New York: Vintage Books,
             1956, pp. 3-15.
           <u>CSF</u>, pp. 69-77.

[1909]
May   22   "The Palatine / (In the 'Dark Ages')."
            Poem. New York Times Saturday Review
            14:317.
            McClure's 33 (June 1909):158-59.
            Paine, Albert Bigelow. Mark Twain: A
              Biography. New York: Harper, 1912.
              Vol. 3:1501-1502. [First three stanzas
              only.]
            The New Poetry: An Anthology of Twentieth
              Century Verse in English. Edited by
              Harriet Monroe and Alice Corbin Hender-
              son. New York: The Macmillan Company,
              1917, pp. 43-44.
            ATOP, pp. 47-48.
            Library ed. 3:185.

Aug.   Introduction to "Four Years in the Schlues-
            selburg Fortress" by I. P. Youvatshev.
            McClure's 33:399-400. [Signed only
            "Editor," but a holograph manuscript in
            Colby Library is signed Willa Sibert
            Cather.]

Dec.   Introduction to "The Secrets of the Sch-
            luesselburg: Chapters from the Secret
            History of Russia's Most Terrible Poli-
            tical Prison" by David Soskice. McClure's
            34:144-45.

1911
Sept.   "The Swedish Mother / (Nebraska)." Poem.
            McClure's 37:541.
            ATOP, pp. 52-53.
            Library ed. 3:192-94.

Oct.   "The Joy of Nelly Deane." Short story.
            Century 82:859-67.
            CSF, pp. 55-68.

89

1912
Feb.

Alexander's Masquerade. Novel. McClure's
38(February, March, April):384-95, 523-
36, 658-68. [Retitled Alexander's Bridge;
see next entry.]

Apr.

Alexander's Bridge. Novel. Boston: Houghton
Mifflin Co.

Edition with a preface by the author.
Boston: Houghton Mifflin Co., 1922.

Golden Book 18 (October, November, December 1933):289-302, 467-80, 559-75.

Library ed. 3:1-137.

Reprinted with the preface of 1922. New
York: Bantam Books, 1962.

May

"Behind the Singer Tower." Short story.
Collier's 49:16-17, 41.
CSF, pp. 43-54.

June

"Spanish Johnny." Poem. McClure's 39:204.
The New Poetry: An Anthology of Twentieth
Century Verse in English. Edited by
Harriet Monroe and Alice Corbin Hender-
son. New York: The Macmillan Company,
1917, pp. 44-45.
ATOP, p. 54.
Literary Digest 78 (21 July 1923):34.
American Ballads and Folk Songs. Compiled
by John A. and Alan Lomax. New York:
The Macmillan Company, 1934. [As a song
with music by Charles Elbert Scoggins.]
Library ed. 3:195-96.
As a song with music by Elmo Russ. New
York: U. S. Music, Inc., 1940.
As a song with music by John Charles
Sacco. New York: G. Schirmer, Inc.,

[1912]   1941.
                Sergeant, Elizabeth Shepley. Willa Ca-
                    ther: A Memoir. Revised ed. Lincoln:
                    University of Nebraska Press, 1963,
                    pp. 183-84.

Aug.   "The Bohemian Girl." Short story. McClure's
                    39: 420-43.
                    CSF, pp. 3-41.

Dec.   "Prairie Spring." Poem. McClure's 40:226.
                    O Pioneers! Boston: Houghton Mifflin
                        Company, 1913, epigraph.
                    NSJ, 10 June 1917, p. 3-C.
                    ATOP, p. 56.
                    Library ed. 3:198.
                    Sergeant, Elizabeth Shepley. Willa Ca-
                        ther: A Memoir. Revised ed. Lincoln:
                        University of Nebraska Press, 1963,
                        pp. 84-85.

1913
Mar.   "Plays of Real Life." Article. McClure's
                    40:63-72.

June   McClure, Samuel Sidney. My Autobiography.
                    McClure's 41:33-35; McClure's 42 (July,
                    August, September, October, November,
                    December 1913):78-87, 95-108, 96-108,
                    76-87, 95-108, 85-95; McClure's 43
                    (January, February 1914):137-54, 120-
                    28. [Recognized and accepted as Willa
                    Cather's work.]
                    Published as a book. New York: Fred-
                        erick A. Stokes Co., [c. 1914].

                O Pioneers! Novel. Illustrated by Clarence
                    F. Underwood. Boston: Houghton Mifflin
                    Co.

[1913]   Edition with a preface. Boston: Houghton
             Mifflin Co., 1923.

             Riverside Library ed. Boston: Houghton
             Mifflin Co., 1929.

             Library ed. Vol. 1.

             Edition for the Armed Services, Inc., no.
             823.

             Sentry ed. Boston: Houghton Mifflin Co.,
             [1961].

             Large type ed. New York: Franklin Watts,
             [1966].

Oct.   "Training for the Ballet: Making American
             Dancers." Article. McClure's 41:85-95.

Dec.   "Three American Singers." Article. Mc-
             Clure's 42:33-48.

             "A Likeness / (Portrait Bust of an Unknown,
             Capitol, Rome.)" Poem. Scribner's Maga-
             zine 54:711-12.
             Anthology of Magazine Verse for 1913.
                Edited by William Stanley Braithwaite.
                Cambridge, Massachusetts: W. S. B.,
                1914, pp. 46-47.
             Literary Digest 48 (31 January 1914):219.
             NSJ, 6 February 1914, p. 12.
             ATOP, pp. 50-51.
             Library ed. 3:189-91.

             "The Dead Forerunner." Poem. Signed "C. W."
             Scribner's Magazine 54:743.

1914   McClure, Samuel Sidney. My Autobiography.
             New York: Frederick A. Stokes Co.,

                              92

[1914]   [c. 1914]. [Recognized and accepted
              as Willa Cather's work.]

              Special ed. for the inspiration of the
              Field Secretaries of Lewis E. Myers & Co.
              New York: Magazine Publishers, 1914.

Feb.   "New Types of Acting: the Character Actor
              Displaces the Star." Article. McClure's
              42:41-51.

1915
Jan.   "The Sweated Drama." Article. McClure's
              44:17-28.

May   "Street in Packingtown." Poem. Century
              Magazine 90:23.
              ATOP, pp. 60-61.
              Library ed. 3:203-204.

Aug.   2   "Wireless Boys Who Went Down with Their
              Ships." Article. Every Week 14:1.

Oct.   ["On Uplands."] Poem as dedication. The
              Song of the Lark. Boston: Houghton
              Mifflin Company.
              Sergeant, Elizabeth Shepley. Willa Ca-
                  ther: A Memoir. Revised ed. Lincoln:
                  University of Nebraska Press, 1963,
                  p. 26.
              Brown, E. K. Willa Cather. New York:
                  Alfred A. Knopf, 1953, p. 97.

              The Song of the Lark. Novel. Boston:
                  Houghton Mifflin Co.

              An edition revised and shortened and
              with a preface. Boston: Houghton
              Mifflin Co., 1932.

[1915]   Library ed. Vol. 2.

                Sentry ed. Boston: Houghton Mifflin
                Co., 1943.

Nov.   "Consequences." Short story. <u>McClure's</u>
                46:30-32, 63-64.
                <u>UV</u>, pp. 67-84.

1916
May   "The Bookkeeper's Wife." Short story.
                <u>Century</u> 92:51-59.
                <u>Golden Book</u> 10 (November 1929):74-78.
                <u>UV</u>, pp. 87-97.

Oct.   "The Diamond Mine." Short story. <u>McClure's</u>
                47:7-11.
                <u>YBM</u>, pp. 79-139.
                Library ed. 6:75-140.

1917
Jan.   "A Gold Slipper." Short story. <u>Harper's</u>
                134:166-74.
                <u>YBM</u>, pp. 140-68.
                <u>Golden Book</u> 3 (March 1926):359-66.
                Library ed. 6:141-72.

1918
May   "Ardessa." Short story. <u>Century</u> 96:105-
                116.
                <u>UV</u>, pp. 101-115.

Oct.   <u>My Ántonia</u>. Novel. Illustrated by W. T.
                Benda. Boston: Houghton Mifflin Co.

                Edition with a revised introduction.
                Boston: Houghton Mifflin Co., [c. 1926].

[1918] "Pavel and Peter: An Incident from My Án-
        tonia." Golden Book 17 (May 1933):459-60.

        Library ed. Vol. 4.

        Edition for the Armed Services, Inc., no.
        G-185.

        Edition with an introduction by Walter
        Havighurst. Boston: Houghton Mifflin Co.,
        [1949].

        Sentry ed. Boston: Houghton Mifflin Co.,
        [1962].

        Large type ed. New York: Franklin Watts,
        [1966].

1919
Aug.   "Roll Call on the Prairies." Article. Red
        Cross Magazine, pp. 27-30.

        "Scandal." Short story. Century 98:433-45.
        YBM, pp. 169-98.
        Library ed. 6:173-205.

Oct.   "Her Boss." Short story. Smart Set 90:95-
        108.
        UV, pp. 119-39.

1920   "On the Art of Fiction." Essay. The Borzoi,
        1920. New York: A. A. Knopf, pp. 7-8.
        OW, pp. 99-104.

Aug.   "Coming, Eden Bower!" Short story. Smart
        Set 92:3-25. [Collected with many
        significant changes and retitled "Coming,
        Aphrodite!"; see that entry below.]
        UV, pp. 143-76. [Smart Set version.]

[1920]

Oct.   <u>Youth</u> <u>and</u> <u>the</u> <u>Bright</u> <u>Medusa</u>. Short story
              collection. New York: Alfred A. Knopf.

            Pocket Book ed. New York: A. A. Knopf,
              1925.

            Library ed. Vol. 6.

            "Coming, Aphrodite!" Short story. <u>YBM</u>,
              pp. 11-78.
              <u>Golden</u> <u>Book</u> 4 (November 1926):591-609.
              Library ed. 6:1-74.
              <u>Coming</u>, <u>Aphrodite!</u> <u>and</u> <u>Other</u> <u>Stories</u>.
                New York: Avon Publications, 1955.

1922

Apr.   12   "The Novel Démeublé." Essay. <u>New</u> <u>Republic</u>
              30:supplement 5-6.
              <u>Modern</u> <u>Essays</u>. Second series. Edited by
                Christopher Morley. New York: Harcourt,
                Brace & Co., 1924, pp. 287-93.
              <u>Book</u> <u>of</u> <u>Modern</u> <u>Essays</u>. Edited by Bruce W.
                McCullough and E. B. Burgum. New York:
                Scribner, [c. 1926], pp. 391-95.
              <u>Facts</u> <u>and</u> <u>Ideas</u> <u>for</u> <u>Students</u> <u>of</u> <u>English</u>
                <u>Composition</u> by John Owen Beaty and
                others. New York: F. S. Crofts & Co.,
                1931, pp. 221-24.
              <u>NUF</u>, pp. 43-51.
              Library ed. 12:233-41.
              <u>OW</u>, pp. 33-43.

Sept.   <u>One</u> <u>of</u> <u>Ours</u>. Novel. Alfred A. Knopf.

            Edition with an introduction by Stanley
            T. Williams. New York: A. A. Knopf, 1926.

            Library ed. Vol. 5.

[1922]   Vintage ed. New York: Alfred A. Knopf,
            Inc., 1971.

Nov.   4 "The House on Charles Street." Part of
            the essay "148 Charles Street." Liter-
            ary Review of the New York Evening Post.
            NUF, pp. 52-75. [Complete essay.]
            Literary ed. 12:243-63. [Complete
              essay.]

Dec.   Book review of Memoirs of a Hostess, a
            Chronicle of Eminent Friendships, drawn
            chiefly from the diaries of Mrs. James
            Fields by Mark A. DeWolfe Howe. Atlantic
            Bookshelf 130.
            Fact, Fancy and Opinion. Edited by Robert
             Malcolm Gay. Boston: Atlantic Monthly
             Press, [c. 1923], pp. 338-40.

1923
Apr.   April Twilights and Other Poems. Poetry
            collection. New York: Alfred A. Knopf,
            Inc.

            Revised ed. New York: Alfred A Knopf,
            Inc., 1933. [Adds one new poem "Poor
            Marty."]

            Library ed. 3:145-217.

            "The Gaul in the Capitol." Poem. ATOP,
             p. 49.
            Library ed. 3:187-88.

            "Macon Prairie." Poem. ATOP, pp. 57-59.
            Library ed. 3:199-202.

            "A Silver Cup." Poem. ATOP, pp. 62-64.
            Library ed. 3:205-208.

[1923]   "Recognition." Poem. <u>ATOP</u>, p. 65.
         Library ed. 3:209.

         "Going Home." Poem. <u>ATOP</u>, p. 66.
         Library ed. 3:216-17.
         Sergeant, Elizabeth Shepley. <u>Willa Ca-</u>
           <u>ther</u>: <u>A Memoir</u>. Revised ed. Lincoln:
           University of Nebraska Press, 1963,
           p. 24. [Third stanza only.]

         <u>A Lost Lady</u>. Novel. <u>Century</u> 105 (April):
         803-822; <u>Century</u> 106 (May, June):73-94,
         289-309.

Sept.   <u>A Lost Lady</u>. Novel. New York: Alfred A.
         Knopf.

         Edition illustrated with scenes from the
         photoplay A Warner Bros. Screen Classic.
         Grosset & Dunlap, [c. 1923].

         <u>Golden Book</u> 14 (September, October,
         November, December 1931):97-110, 280-
         94, 376-89, 463-79.

         Library ed. Vol. 7.

         <u>Fifty Years</u>: <u>Being a Retrospective Col-</u>
         <u>lection</u>. . . . Edited with an introduc-
         tion by Clifton Fadiman. New York: A. A.
         Knopf, 1965, pp. 94-160.

         Vintage ed. New York: Alfred A. Knopf,
         Inc., 1972.

         Centennial ed. designed by Warren Chap-
         pell. New York: Alfred A. Knopf, 1973.

     5 "Nebraska: the End of the First Cycle."
         Article. <u>Nation</u> 117:236-38. [In a
         series "These United States."]

[1923]   Further Adventures in Essay Reading.
                  Edited by Thomas E. Rankin and others.
                  New York: Harcourt, Brace & Co.,
                  [c. 1928], pp. 65-76.
                Modern Writing. Edited by Willard Thorp
                  and M. F. Thorp. New York: American
                  Book Co., [c. 1944], pp. 121-29.
                America is West; an Anthology of Middle-
                  western Life and Literature. Edited by
                  John T. Flanagan. Minneapolis: Univer-
                  sity of Minnesota Press, [1945],
                  pp. 618-25.
                Roundup: A Nebraska Reader. Compiled and
                  edited by Virginia Faulkner. Lincoln:
                  University of Nebraska Press, 1957,
                  pp. 1-8.

1924   Introduction to The Fortunate Mistress by
                  Daniel Defoe. New York: Alfred A. Knopf,
                  pp. vii-xiii.
                OW, pp. 75-88.

1925   "Katherine Mansfield." Essay. The Borzoi,
                  1925: Being a Sort of Record of Ten Years
                  of Publishing. New York: A. A. Knopf,
                  pp. 47-49.
                NUF, pp. 123-47. [Essay much expanded and
                  developed.]
                Library ed. 12:307-328.
                OW, pp. 107-120.

                Preface to The Best Stories of Sarah Orne
                  Jewett. Boston: Houghton Mifflin Co.,
                  pp. ix-xix. [Cather's preface dated
                  February; part of essay repeated in
                  "Miss Jewett," NUF, 1936.]
                Bookman 6 (July 1925):594-95. [Review.]
                OW, pp. 47-59.
                Jewett, Sarah Orne. The Country of the

                                99

[1925]   _Pointed Firs and Other Stories_. Anchor
                 ed. Garden City, N. Y.: Doubleday &
                 Company, Inc., 1956, pp. 6-11.

                 Introduction to _The Wagnerian Romances_ by
                 Gertrude (Hall) Brownell. New York:
                 Alfred A. Knopf, pp. vii-x.
                 _OW_, pp. 60-66.

Feb.   "Uncle Valentine." Short story. _Woman's
                 Home Companion_ 52 (February, March):
                 7-9, 86, 89-90 and 15-16, 75-76, 79-80.
                 _UV_, pp. 3-38.

June   6   _The Professor's House_. Novel. _Collier's_ 75
                 (6, 13, 20, 27 June):5-7, 24-32, 22-23,
                 28-35; _Collier's_ 76 (4, 11, 18, 25 July,
                 1 August):30-35, 24-25, 22-23, 22-23,
                 22-23.

Sept.   _The Professor's House_. Novel. New York:
                 Alfred A. Knopf.

                 Edition. New York: Grosset & Dunlap,
                 [c. 1925].

                 Library ed. Vol. 8.

                 "Tom Outland's Story." Book II of _The
                 Professor's House_. _Five Stories_. New
                 York: Vintage Books, 1956, pp. 16-71.

                 Vintage ed. New York: Alfred A. Knopf,
                 Inc., 1973.

1926   Introduction to "Wounds in the Rain and
                 Other Impressions of War," vol. 9 of
                 The Work of Stephen Crane. New York:
                 Alfred A. Knopf, pp. ix-xiv.
                 _OW_, pp. 67-74.

[1926]
Oct.   My Mortal Enemy. Novel. New York: Alfred
            A. Knopf.

            The Borzoi Reader. Edited with an intro-
            duction and notes by Carl Van Doren.
            New York: A. A. Knopf, 1936, pp. 5-48.

            Library ed. 11:237-329.

            Vintage ed. with an introduction by
            Marcus Klein. New York: Alfred A.
            Knopf, Inc., 1961.

1927
Jan.   Death Comes for the Archbishop. Novel.
            Forum 77 (January, February, March,
            April, May, June):22-29, 286-97, 450-
            61, 612-25, 770-84, 930-42.

Sept.   Death Comes for the Archbishop. Novel.
            New York: Alfred A. Knopf.

            Edition with drawings and designs by von
            Schmidt. New York: Alfred A. Knopf, 1929.

            Modern Library ed. New York: Modern
            Library, Inc., 1931.

            December Night. A scene. New York: A. A.
            Knopf, 1933.

            Large paper ed. with drawings and designs
            by Harold von Schmidt. New York: Alfred
            A. Knopf, 1936.

            Library ed. Vol. 9.

            Edition for the Armed Services, Inc., no.
            D-97.

[1927]   Vintage ed. New York: Alfred A. Knopf,
            Inc., 1971.

Nov. 27 Letter on Death Comes for the Archbishop.
          Commonweal 7:713.
          Willa Cather, a Biographical Sketch; an
            English Opinion. . . . New York: A. A.
            Knopf, 1933.
          OW, pp. 3-13.

1929
Feb.   "Double Birthday." Short story. Forum 81:
            78-82, 124-28.
            Best Short Stories of 1929. Edited by
              Edward J. O'Brien. New York: Dodd,
              Mead & Co., 1929, pp. 60-85.
            A Modern Galaxy. Compiled by Dale Warren.
              New York: Houghton Mifflin & Co., [c.
              1930], pp. 115-55.
            UV, pp. 41-63.

Oct. 27 "Willa Cather Mourns Old Opera House."
            Article. Omaha World-Herald, p. 9.
            Nebraska History 49 (winter 1968):
              373-78. [Titled "The Incomparable
              Opera House" and with a note by
              Mildred R. Bennett.]
            W&P, pp. 955-58.

1930
Apr.   "Neighbor Rosicky." Short story. Woman's
            Home Companion 57 (April, May):7-9, 52,
            54, 57 and 13-14, 92, 95-96. [In all
            collected works the spelling used is
            "Neighbour."]
            OD, pp. 1-71.
            Library ed. 12:7-62.
            Five Stories. New York: Vintage Books,
              1956, pp. 72-111.

1931   The Fear That Walks by Noonday. Story.
        New York: Phoenix Book Shop. [Thirty
        copies.] See "Appendix · Student
        Writing" for 1894.
        Early Stories. Selected by Mildred R.
        Bennett. New York: Dodd, Mead & Co.,
        1957, pp. 45-57.
        CSF, pp. 505-514.

May   "Poor Marty." Poem. Atlantic Monthly 147:
        585-87.
        Literary Digest 109 (9 May 1931):24.
        ATOP. Revised ed., 1933, pp. 67-70.
        Library ed. 3:210-215.

June   "My First Novels (There Were Two)."
        Article. Colophon, part 6, no. 4, 21.
        OW, pp. 89-97.

Aug.   Shadows on the Rock. Novel. New York:
        Alfred A. Knopf.

        Library ed. Vol. 10.

        Vintage ed. New York: Alfred A. Knopf,
        Inc., 1971.

Oct. 17 Letter to Governor Wilbur Cross on Shadows
        on the Rock. Saturday Review of Litera-
        ture 8:216.
        Willa Cather, a Biographical Sketch; an
        English Opinion. . . . New York: A. A.
        Knopf, 1933.
        Designed for Reading. Edited by H. S.
        Canby and others. New York: Macmillan
        Co., 1934, pp. 596-98.
        OW, pp. 14-17.

1932

July   "Two Friends." Short story. Woman's
             Home Companion. 59:7-9, 54-56.
             OD, pp. 191-230.
             Library ed. 12:159-91.

Aug.   Obscure Destinies. Short story collection.
             New York: Alfred A. Knopf.

             Library ed. 12:7-191.

             Vintage ed. New York: Alfred A. Knopf,
             Inc., 1974.

             "Old Mrs. Harris." Short story. OD, pp. 73-
             190.
               Ladies' Home Journal 49 (September, Octo-
                 ber, November):3, 70, 72, 74, 76-77;
                 18, 85-87; 16, 84-85, 89. [Magazine
                 version titled "Three Women."]
               Library ed. 12:63-158.

             "Three Women." See "Old Mrs. Harris" above.

1933

Feb.   "A Chance Meeting." Essay. Atlantic Monthly
             151:154-65.
             NUF, pp. 3-42.
             Library ed. 12:197-231.

May   "Pavel and Peter." An "incident" from My
             Ántonia. Golden Book 17:459-60.

             December Night. A scene from Death Comes
             for the Archbishop. New York: A. A.
             Knopf.

1935

Feb.   Lucy Gayheart. Novel. New York: Alfred A.

[1935]   Knopf.

            <u>Woman's</u> <u>Home</u> <u>Companion</u> 62 (March, April,
            May, June, July):7-10, 14-17, 23-26, 16-
            18, 15-17.

            Library ed. 11:3-234.

1936
Apr.   17   "Escapism, a letter to <u>The</u> <u>Commonweal</u>."
            <u>Commonweal</u> 23:677-79.
            <u>OW</u>, pp. 18-29.

June   6   "The Birth of Personality: an Appreciation
            of Thomas Mann's Trilogy." <u>Saturday</u>
            <u>Review</u> of <u>Literature</u> 14:3-4. [Printed
            as "Joseph and His Brothers" in later
            publication.]
            <u>NUF</u>, pp. 96-122.
            Library ed. 12:283-306.

Nov.   <u>Not</u> <u>Under</u> <u>Forty</u>. Collection of essays. New
            York: Alfred A. Knopf.

            Library ed. 12:193-328. [Retitled
            <u>Literary</u> <u>Encounters</u>.]

            "Miss Jewett." <u>NUF</u>, pp. 76-95. [Part of
            this sketch was the preface to the
            Jewett collection, 1925.]
            Library ed. 12:265-82.

            "Joseph and His Brothers." See "The Birth
            of Personality" above.

1937   <u>The</u> <u>Novels</u> <u>and</u> <u>Stories</u> <u>of</u> <u>Willa</u> <u>Cather</u>.
            Collected works. Boston: Houghton Mifflin
            Co., 1937-1941, 13 vols. Library ed. and
            simultaneously issued in a limited Auto-

                              105

[1937]   graph Ed.

                Literary Encounters; see Not Under Forty,
                     November 1936.

1940   "Portrait of the Publisher [Alfred A.
                     Knopf] As a Young Man." Article. Alfred
                     A. Knopf Quarter Century. New York:
                     Plimpton Press, pp. 9-16.

Dec.   Sapphira and the Slave Girl. Novel. New
                     York: Alfred A. Knopf.

                Library ed. Vol. 13.

1948   "Shakespeare / A Freshman Theme." Poem.
                     "Willa Cather Juvenilia," edited by
                     James R. Shively. Prairie Schooner 22:
                     98-99.
                     "Willa Cather, Undergraduate," by John
                          P. Hinz. American Literature 21 (March
                          1949):112-13.
                     CY, pp. 109-110.
                     AT3. Revised ed., pp. 61-62.

                "Columbus." Poem. "Willa Cather Juvenilia,"
                     edited by James R. Shively. Prairie
                     Schooner 22:99-100.
                     "Willa Cather, Undergraduate," by John
                          P. Hinz. American Literature 21 (March
                          1949):114-15.
                     CY, p. 111.
                     AT3. Revised ed., p. 63.

                "Lou, the Prophet." Short story. "Willa
                     Cather Juvenilia," edited by James R.
                     Shively. Prairie Schooner 22:100-104.
                     CY, pp. 46-53.
                     Early Stories. Selected by Mildred R.

[1948]   Bennett. New York: Dodd, Mead & Co.,
                1957, pp. 9-17.
                CSF, pp. 535-40.

                "The Clemency of the Court." Short story.
                "Willa Cather's Juvenilia," edited by
                James R. Shively. Prairie Schooner 22:
                104-111.
                CY, pp. 69-79.
                Early Stories. Selected by Mildred R.
                  Bennett. New York: Dodd, Mead & Co.,
                  1957, pp. 33-43.
                CSF, pp. 515-522.

Sept.   The Old Beauty, and Others. Short story
                collection. New York: Alfred A. Knopf.

                "The Old Beauty." Short story. The Old
                Beauty, and Others. New York: Alfred A.
                Knopf, pp. 3-72.

                "The Best Years." Short story. The Old
                Beauty, and Others. New York: Alfred A.
                Knopf, pp. 73-138.
                Five Stories. New York: Vintage Books,
                  1956, pp. 112-48.

                "Before Breakfast." Short story. The Old
                Beauty, and Others. New York: Alfred A.
                Knopf, pp. 141-66.

1949
Sept.   Willa Cather on Writing: Critical Studies
                on Writing As an Art. Collection of
                letters and essays. Foreword by Stephen
                Tennant. New York: Alfred A. Knopf.

                Letter on The Professor's House. OW
                pp. 30-32. [Letter is dated 12 December
                1938.]

[1949]   "Light on Adobe Walls." A Fragment. <u>OW</u>,
            pp. 123-26.

1950   <u>Writings</u> <u>from</u> <u>Willa</u> <u>Cather's</u> <u>Campus</u> <u>Years</u>.
            Miscellany. Edited by James R. Shively.
            Lincoln: University of Nebraska Press.

          "A Tale of the White Pyramid." Short story.
            <u>CY</u>, pp. 54-60.
            <u>Early</u> <u>Stories</u>. Selected by Mildred R.
              Bennett. New York: Dodd, Mead & Co.,
              1957, pp. 19-24.
            <u>CSF</u>, pp. 529-33.

          "[Ah Lie Me Dead in the Sunrise Land.]" Poem
            with the short story "A Son of the Celes-
            tial." <u>CY</u>, p. 61.
            <u>Early</u> <u>Stories</u>. Selected by Mildred R.
              Bennett. New York: Dodd, Mead & Co.,
              1957, pp. 25-26.
            <u>CSF</u>, p. 523.

          "A Son of the Celestial." Short story. <u>CY</u>,
            pp. 61-68.
            <u>Early</u> <u>Stories</u>. Selected by Mildred R.
              Bennett. New York: Dodd, Mead & Co.,
              1957, pp. 25-32.
            <u>CSF</u>, pp. 523-28.

          "Daily Dialogues or, Cloak Room Conversa-
            tion as Overheard by the Tired Listener."
            Play. <u>CY</u>, pp. 93-99.

          "A Sentimental Thanksgiving Dinner In Five
            Courses." Play. <u>CY</u>, pp. 100-108.

          "Anacreon." Poem. <u>CY</u>, p. 110.

          "Horace / Book I, Ode XXXVIII / 'Persicos

[1950]   Odi.''' Translation of a poem. CY, p. 112.

1956
Feb.   Five Stories, with an article by George
              N. Kates on Miss Cather's last, un-
              finished, and unpublished Avignon story.
              New York: Vintage Books.

              Willa Cather in Europe, Her Own Story of
              the First Journey. With an Introduction
              and Incidental Notes by George N. Kates.
              New York: Alfred A. Knopf. [Kates's
              introduction dated April.]

1957   Early Stories of Willa Cather. Selected
              and with commentary by Mildred R.
              Bennett. New York: Dodd, Mead & Com-
              pany.

1962
June   April Twilights (1903), Poems by Willa
              Cather. Edited with an introduction by
              Bernice Slote. Lincoln: University of
              Nebraska Press.

              Revised ed. Lincoln: University of
              Nebraska Press, 1968.

1965
July   Willa Cather's Collected Short Fiction,
              1892-1912. [Edited by Virginia Faulkner.]
              Introduction by Mildred R. Bennett. Lin-
              coln: University of Nebraska Press.

              Revised ed. Edited by Virginia Faulkner,
              introduction by Mildred R. Bennett.
              Lincoln: University of Nebraska Press,

[1965]   November 1970.

1966   The Kingdom of Art: Willa Cather's First
             Principles and Critical Statements, 1893-
             1896. Selected and edited with two essays
             and a commentary by Bernice Slote. Lin-
             coln: University of Nebraska Press.
             [Although the copyright date is listed as
             1966, the book was not issued until 4
             January 1967.]

             Editorial comment on the Lansing curtain.
             KA, pp. 173-74.

             Editorial comment on football. KA, p. 212.

             "The Elopement of Allen Poole." Short
             story. KA, pp. 437-41.

1968   "The Easter Rabbit." Poem. Handwritten
             and subtitled "Respectfully Dedicated
             to Miss Elsie Cather on the Ides of
             March 1896." Willa Cather Pioneer
             Memorial and Educational Foundation
             Newsletter 12 (spring):1.

1970
Dec.   The World and the Parish: Willa Cather's
             Articles and Reviews, 1893-1902. Selected
             and edited with a commentary by William
             M. Curtin. 2 vols. Lincoln: University
             of Nebraska Press.

             In "Pastels in Prose" a sketch of Roscoe
             Pound. W&P, p. 122.

1973
Feb.   <u>Uncle Valentine and Other Stories: Willa
Cather's Uncollected Short Fiction, 1915–
1929</u>. Edited with an introduction by
Bernice Slote. Lincoln: University of
Nebraska Press.

APPENDIX · STUDENT WRITING

1891
Mar.   1   "Literary." Essay on Thomas Carlyle.
            Unsigned. Hesperian, pp. 4-5.
            NSJ, 1 March 1891, p. 14. [Edited
               and revised; see KA, p. 421.]
            KA, pp. 421-25. [Hesperian version.]

1892
June   1   "Shakespeare / A Freshman Theme." Poem.
            Signed W. Cather. Hesperian, p. 3.
            "Willa Cather Juvenilia," edited by
               James R. Shively. Prairie Schooner
               22 (spring 1948):98-99.
            "Willa Cather, Undergraduate," by
               John P. Hinz. American Literature
               21 (March 1949):112-13.
            CY, pp. 109-110.
            AT3. Revised ed., p. 61-62.

Oct.   15   "Lou, the Prophet." Short story. Signed
            W. Cather. Hesperian, pp. 7-10.
            "Willa Cather Juvenilia," edited by
               James R. Shively. Prairie Schooner
               22 (spring 1948):100-104.
            CY, pp. 46-53.
            Early Stories. Selected by Mildred R.
               Bennett. New York: Dodd, Mead & Co.,
               1957, pp. 9-17.
            CSF, pp. 535-40.

Nov.   1   "Columbus." Poem. Signed W. Cather. Hes-
            perian, p. 9.
            "Willa Cather Juvenilia," edited by
               James R. Shively. Prairie Schooner
               22 (spring 1948):99-100.
            "Willa Cather, Undergraduate," by John
               P. Hinz. American Literature 21 (March
               1949):114-15.
            CY, p. 111.
            AT3. Revised ed., p. 63.

[1892]

24   "A Sentimental Thanksgiving Dinner in Five
       Courses." Play. Signed W. Cather. Hes-
       perian, pp. 4-7.
       CY, pp. 100-108.

     "Peter." Short story. Signed Willa Cather.
       Hesperian, pp. 10-12.
       Mahogany Tree, 21 May 1892, pp. 323-24.
         [Original version; Hesperian version
         has sixteen changes.]
       Library, 21 July 1900, p. 5. [Retitled
         "Peter Sadelack, Father of Anton" and
         revised, with additional alterations
         from the Hesperian version.]
       CY, pp. 41-45. [Hesperian version.]
       Early Stories. Selected by Mildred R.
         Bennett. New York: Dodd, Mead & Co.,
         1957, pp. 1-8. [Mahogany Tree and
         Hesperian versions.]
       CSF, pp. 541-43. [Mahogany Tree version.]

     "Horace / Book I, Ode XXXVIII / 'Persicos
       Odi.'" Translation of a poem. Signed W.
       Cather. Hesperian, p. 12.
       CY, p. 112.

Dec. 22 "A Tale of the White Pyramid." Short story.
           Signed W. Cather. Hesperian, pp. 8-11.
           CY, pp. 54-60.
           Early Stories. Selected by Mildred R.
             Bennett. New York: Dodd, Mead & Co.,
             1957, pp. 19-24.
           CSF, pp. 529-33.

1893
Jan. 15 "[Ah Lie Me Dead in the Sunrise Land.]" Poem
           with the short story "A Son of the Celes-
           tial." Signed W. Cather. Hesperian, p. 7.
           CY, p. 61.

[1893]   Early Stories. Selected by Mildred R.
                   Bennett. New York: Dodd, Mead & Co.,
                   1957, pp. 25-26.
                CSF, p. 523.

                "A Son of the Celestial." Short story.
                Signed W. Cather. Hesperian, pp. 7-10.
                CY, pp. 61-68.
                Early Stories. Selected by Mildred R.
                   Bennett. New York: Dodd, Mead & Co.,
                   1957, pp. 25-32.
                CSF, pp. 523-28.

Feb.   15   "Daily Dialogues or, Cloak Room Conversa-
                tion as Overheard by the Tired Listener."
                Play. Signed W. C. Hesperian, pp. 3-5.
                CY, pp. 93-99.

Mar.   15   Editorial comment on the Lansing curtain.
                Unsigned. Hesperian, p. 3.
                KA, pp. 173-74.

Apr.   15   "The Elopement of Allen Poole." Short
                story. Unsigned. Hesperian, pp. 4-7.
                KA, pp. 437-41.

Oct.   26   "The Clemency of the Court." Short story.
                Signed W. Cather. Hesperian, pp. 3-7.
                "Willa Cather Juvenilia," edited by
                   James R. Shively. Prairie Schooner
                   22 (spring 1948):104-111.
                CY, pp. 69-79.
                Early Stories. Selected by Mildred R.
                   Bennett. New York: Dodd, Mead & Co.,
                   1957, pp. 33-43.
                CSF, pp. 515-22.

Nov.   15   Editorial comment on football. Unsigned.
                Hesperian, p. 9.
                KA, p. 212.

1894   "Anacreon." Poem. Signed W. C. <u>Sombrero</u>,
           p. 222.
           <u>CY</u>, p. 110.

       "The Fear That Walks by Noonday." Short
           story. Signed Willa Cather and Dorothy
           Canfield. <u>Sombrero</u>, pp. 224-31. [The
           idea for the story was suggested to
           Willa Cather by Dorothy Canfield.]
           Thirty copies published as a book.
             New York: Phoenix Book Shop, 1931.
           <u>Early Stories</u>. Selected by Mildred R.
             Bennett. New York: Dodd, Mead & Co.,
             1957, pp. 45-57.
           <u>CSF</u>, pp. 505-514.

Mar. 10 In "Pastels in Prose" a sketch of Roscoe
           Pound. Unsigned. <u>Hesperian</u>, pp. 4-5.
           <u>W&P</u>, p. 122.

16